ETERNALLY
awkward

A Future Mom of Eight Reflects on Mysteries
of Anxiety, ADHD, and Coming of Age
in the '80s

by Amy Liz Harrison

Eternally Awkward
Copyright ©2022 by Amy Liz Harrison

Published by
A Team Press

ISBN: 979-8-9856945-0-5
eISBN: 979-8-9856945-1-2
Audio Book ISBN: 979-8-9856945-2-9

Original Cover Concept by Amy Liz Harrison
Developmental and Copyediting by Becky J. Sasso
Proofreading by Kim Bookless
Cover and Interior Design by GKS Creative
Cover Photo by Carolyn Bunn
Author Photo by Toni Pinto
Project Management by The Cadence Group

Images contained in this work have been released by Dohm Design Company for the exclusive use of Amy Liz Harrison. This book may contain copyrighted content not authorized for use by the owner. The use of such content falls under the guidelines of fair use per Section 107 of the Copyright Act.

All Rights Reserved. No part of this book may be reproduced or transmitted in any form or by any means, electronic or mechanical, including photocopying, recording, or by any information retrieval or storage system, without the prior written consent of the publisher.

This work is nonfiction and, as such, reflects the author's memory of her experiences. Many of the names and identifying characteristics of the individuals featured in this book have been changed to protect their privacy, and certain individuals are composites. Exact dialogue and accuracy of some events have been recreated to show the idea of what happened from the author's perspective. In some cases, conversations have been edited or slightly altered to convey their substance rather than written exactly as they occurred.

Dedicated to:
Obviously, the A-Team: Like Madonna, ya know I'm crazy for you!

TOTALLY Dedicated to:
The Weirdos, Nerds, and Misfits of Generation X. You are my people.

SO TOTALLY Dedicated to:
Be Fri. Thanks for appreciating my brand of crazy.
WE ARE the MOST FUN EVER! Love you long time—St Ends

TOTALLY NOT Dedicated to:
The Down Girls

PS to Annie:
What can I say? We never made out. Sorry not sorry.

contents

Intro
Surveying the Scene   1
A broad view, surveying all the parts,
features, and contents of the vicinity

chapter one
Victims & Casualties   7
Recipients of unfortunate happenings and
occurrences from adverse circumstances

chapter two
Criminals & Culprits   13
Guilty party associated with being
responsible for a criminal offense

chapter three
APBs & BOLOs   25
APBs (All-Points Bulletins) and BOLOs
(Be on the Lookouts) are urgent announcements
and updated notifications among police agencies
containing details of an active situation

chapter four
Badge Bunnies & Holster Sniffers   39
Slang for a certain type of individual whose
personal appearance and behavior is aimed
toward attracting a police officer

chapter five
Interviews & Interrogations   49
Eliciting information and gathering
facts germane to the case

chapter six
Investigation & Scrutinization   61
Careful examination of the
information to solidify facts

chapter seven
Calling for Backup   73
Enlisting the assistance of others

chapter eight
Probable Cause & Reasonable Suspicion   85
Collecting clues and identifying suspects
for the purpose of building a case

chapter nine
Motive & Opportunity   97
Identifying possible suspects
based on mounting evidence

chapter ten
Partners & Squads   105
Sharing resources and expertise
as a community

epilogue
Hook 'Em & Book 'Em   117
Arresting perpetrators based
on probable cause

Activity Pages   119

About the Author   131

Intro

Surveying the Scene

A broad view, surveying all the parts, features, and contents of the vicinity

In slow-motion, the two detectives lurched from the roof of a building, windmilling their arms, free-falling. They tumbled through the air for an unbelievably long time, silhouetted against the Los Angeles skyline, eventually plummeting into a conveniently located swimming pool below.

The year is 1987, it's Tuesday night, and I'm glued to *Moonlighting* on our family's nineteen-inch, remote-less TV set. I shove a handful of microwave popcorn into my mouth without breaking my gaze, which is locked on the screen.

I grew up in California in the 1980s. The loud and proud, definitely *not* forgotten Generation X. Generally speaking, our parents neither monitored screen time nor filtered the content coming through the tube. If you were south of junior high school age, so long as you weren't caught watching MTV or some steamy make out scene on *Guiding Light*, you were safe. Detective shows were all the rage, and my favorite was *Moonlighting*.

Soaked and dripping, Maddie and David scrambled from the pool. They slunk out of the perpetrator's backyard in their underwear, hastily making their seminude escape. Upon reaching the vehicle, they jumped in, shivering, and slammed the car doors behind them. Wrapping up the ever-present bickering, bantering, and sexual tension for the night, they turned to look at each other. David smiled at Maddie and told her that "wet becomes her."

Those little innuendos went right over my head. At the age of ten, I was completely oblivious to the adult world. Rather than being practically raised by search engines and possessing an encyclopedic knowledge of TikTok dances, '80s kids had it easy. We had no reason to doubt those words could have had a different meaning other than face value.

Even if we were suspicious about grown-up things, what were we going to do? Look it up in the dictionary? Call the operator and ask? Really, the best we could hope for was that somebody's older sibling would explain it.

When they did, we would scrunch up our faces, shake our heads, and say, "Gag me with a spoon," or "Grody to the *MAX*!" We were convinced all older siblings were class A perverts.

In many ways, we were living in simpler times.

By today's parenting standards, the world of my youth was a total death trap—full of tires leaking chemicals and sharp metal playground equipment painted with toxic lead paint. Kids who survived the '80s remember riding in the "way back" of the station wagon with no seat belts, scalding our thighs on hot metal slides, and having our first experiences with claustrophobia being trapped in the pee-smelling Hamburglar jails at McDonald's Playlands. I don't think '80s parents were plagued by messages about their kids' constant imminent danger and death the way we are today.

Swimming pools with safety fences? *Pshaw.*

When I was a little less than a year old, I fell into the swimming pool in my grandparents' backyard in Marin County. According to my mom, who was a first-time, overachieving mother, my life was spared because she had already taken me to infant swimming lessons. Those who know my mom will not be surprised by this. As former president of the local school board, she's headed countless safety committees. To this day, she is well-versed in earthquake preparedness and serves as the self-appointed chief of bike helmet safety enforcement. In this role, she feels compelled to blow the whistle and call the parents of any helmetless kids caught riding bikes down the street and minding their own business.

Allegedly, my nine-month-old body immediately popped up like a cork. As the story goes, I proceeded to flip onto my back, take a breath, spread my arms and legs like a starfish, and float. Presumably the adults, who were probably drinking dry Chardonnay and watching golf, just scooped me out of the pool, wrapped me up in a crochet dish towel, and turned up the Doobie Brothers. Simpler times.

Growing up, my mom always had an Agatha Christie novel on her bedside table, so a taste for mystery runs in the family line apparently. Reflecting now, I'm reminded just how many of life's mysteries growing up turned out to make total sense from the vantage point of hindsight.

Especially life seasons of death and rebirth, ends and beginnings.

At the time of this writing, I am surfacing after a twenty-year career as a stay-at-home mom. I feel like someone put me in a time capsule back in 2001, when my first daughter was born, and dropped me like an anchor to the ocean floor. Interestingly, 2001 was also the year Michael Jackson released his song "Heaven Can Wait."

Some have said that in this song, Michael predicts his untimely death in 2009. Others have said the song is an analogy of the crucifixion of

Christ and Jesus' love for Mary Magdalene. In either scenario, it's about a desire to avoid death to be with the one he loves.

There is a scene in the video where Michael is standing waist-deep in a river in front of a waterfall, wearing a pair of angel wings. In a sense, 2001 was the death of the first versions of myself, so that I could be reborn into my next chapter as a mother. Look, I realize my pop culture references are old, I don't know how to utilize half of the tools on my iPhone, and I still use a desktop thesaurus. When I write, I basically look around for my Apple IIe computer and a floppy disk.

My first book, *Eternally Expecting*, explored my adult life before and after parenthood, equating my recovery from alcoholism with the process of gestation and childbirth. I am intimately acquainted with this process after enduring eight pregnancies and the eight subsequent births. But my first book didn't devote much airtime to my early life. My Aqua Net–drenched (Has anyone ever thought to call it "Awkward" Net?) elementary school days in the 1980s led to community theater hijinks in junior high, church youth group shenanigans, and general incidents of high school tomfoolery. The '90s brought me back to LA for college, where I fancied myself a wannabe Stacy Sheridan in *T. J. Hooker* when I was commissioned as a Campus Safety Officer, AKA university rent-a-cop. Cue laughter.

Like many kids, I started life pretty sure of myself and excited about who I would become. Then things started to get complicated. Puberty felt uncontrolled and reckless—I had the sense of freefalling just like Maddie and David in that *Moonlighting* episode. I convinced myself life would be complete if I were to wake up and discover I was Maddie Hayes in *Moonlighting*: sophisticated, poised, and independent.

Now that I'm sober, I'm learning to accept and embrace every part of myself. Reflecting on my youthful attempts to avoid awkwardness, one watershed incident has stayed with me all this time. It became the foundation of this book.

I know now it was my first anxiety attack.

As you might suspect from the title of this book, my awkwardness eclipsed my hope of being poised and put together like Maddie from *Moonlighting*. From early childhood through teenage years to college, my tendency to embarrass myself remained consistent. One of the first, and most dramatic, examples of my talent for uncomfortable situations involved CPR certification at school and a dummy named Annie.

I have replayed and pondered the significance of this anxiety attack from time to time, perusing the high-level details of the case. Having been a Michael Jackson fan for as long as I can remember, I was fascinated and dumbfounded when he released the short film and song "Smooth Criminal" in 1987, not long after the incident in question. I was shocked to hear the now familiar refrain of the chorus of "Smooth Criminal": *"Annie, are you okay? . . . Are you okay, Annie?"* The exact words I was supposed to use in class that day before beginning CPR on Annie, the mannequin.

Since that time, in my mind, panic, anxiety, and awkwardness became inextricably linked to this phrase. Yet, until now, its true significance as it pertains to my life remained, like the '80s show hosted by Robert Stack, an unsolved mystery.

Always an amateur sleuth, I've uncovered many truths about myself. Over time, you get the fuller picture of why you do what you do. This creates an understanding of self, which offers an opportunity for self-acceptance. In my case, at least, this principle isn't a linear process—it's cyclical. It needs to be rebirthed often.

Recently, it was time for me to explore a deeper level of self-acceptance. Time to understand this connection between Annie and me, to get below the surface and investigate. Why was this particular panic attack, from memory, my very first one, seemingly so significant in my life? What was I supposed to learn about it?

I suddenly found myself in the middle of my own personal mystery. Like any good detective, I started by asking a few questions.

Why was it that somehow, across the time and space and span of thirty-five years, the incident between myself and Annie, the CPR dummy, was never far from my mind? What did Annie have to teach me about who I was? I was drawn to uncover this story like the magnetic force of the ocean's pull, dragging me out to sea.

To understand the connection involving Annie, I had to rewind the VHS tape all the way to the beginning of her story and mine. As if I were in a trance, I dove into the deep, scraping the seabed, gathering everything I could about Annie. Once I got connected to Annie and swam with her beneath the surface of the waters, it became clear, as my research on the proverbial ocean floor led to treasure.

First to rise to the surface was the gem that the CPR dummy, Annie, I encountered in the 1980s was derived from a young Parisian woman a century earlier...

So go rifle through your closet and find your snorkel gear; we've got some diving to do. We will solve the mystery of why we tend to be so uncomfortable with of some of our awkwardness by holding a magnifying glass up to some of my most embarrassing moments (c'mon, I know you've had yours too) and we'll see how this puzzle fits together, if we take it one piece, one clue at a time. And maybe you, too, will find connection to Annie and some of her secrets.

So grab my hand... because you *know* we both look awkward AF in snorkel gear anyway.

chapter one

Victims & Casualties

Recipients of unfortunate happenings and occurrences from adverse circumstances

"Annie, are you okay?" a middle-aged woman yelled into the face of the rubber dummy at the front of my fourth-grade class. It was just a head with a torso, really. Wearing a shabby red Adidas warmup jacket.

Shifting my weight back and forth, I averted my eyes, staring down at my pink Zips sneakers. There was a dull hum of general background noise. Lighthearted chatter, side comments, and the usual classroom antics: Allen Dixon, in the lime-green OP T-shirt he had worn approximately 874,993 times, made a low comment as he inched closer to Ryan Navsgaard, who flipped the mustard mop masquerading as a shag haircut. The two of them erupted in raucous laughter. Karla Watson was studiously French braiding Jennifer Graves' dishwater blonde hair. Lisa Stoffler was playing with the frosty peach mini wet *n* wild lipstick attached to her plastic charm bracelet.

One by one, they took turns stepping up to Annie lying on the Formica table. We were learning CPR, taking turns practicing chest compressions and rescue breathing. I watched in horror as each of them bent forward. The background noise faded away, and all I could hear was the whoosh of my classmates' breath into manufactured lungs.

My stomach flipped. Maybe I should go to the bathroom. Maybe I needed a drink of water. I turned around to find Janelle Thorndike behind me. She was meticulously cutting her split ends with a pair of nail clippers, which struck me as next-level gross. I wondered if her dad used those same clippers on his toenails. What would possess her to use them on her hair? I gulped and let my eyes fall back to my Zips. The generic beige-and-gray-spotted school tile felt oddly wobbly under my feet.

"Next!" My head snapped back upright. The Red Cross instructor named JoAnne (with an "E," she reminded us repeatedly) was making aggressive motions with her arm, as if she were directing traffic at Candlestick Park after a 49ers game. Her half-gray-half-blonde Arnold Palmer-esque ponytail swished in time with her arm motions.

The single-file line shuffled closer to the tabletop demonstration at the front of the room. I counted the heads in front of me, inching ever closer to my impending doom. Five 1980s haircuts on my fourth-grade classmates, plus Ryan's mustard shag, and it would be my turn. My heart started to pound. Why did the line seem like that last bit of toilet paper nearing the end of the roll, picking up speed and going faster than it should?

In what felt like seconds later, those five haircuts were gone, safely reseated at their desks, chatting and giggling. Ryan's shaggy mustard mop fell around the sides of his face as he bent down over the tabletop torso. *Whoosh!* The sound of Ryan's breath flowing into the latex mannequin resounded in my whole body, and my knees began to shake. I spun around and grabbed Janelle's shoulders.

She stared at me, wide-eyed, and I snatched the disgusting toenail clippers from her hand. "Go ahead, Janelle!" I squeaked, shoving her in front of me.

"Um, okaaay." Janelle shrugged. Ryan was just finishing his chest compressions as evidenced by the sound of the clicking on the artificial diaphragm. Ryan stood upright, flipped his hair, and headed back to his seat.

"Nice job, Ryan," said JoAnne with an E in a satisfied tone.

Janelle approached the torso and shook its shoulder. "Are you okay?" she asked Annie in a dull voice with minimal enthusiasm. The smell of rubbing alcohol filled the air as JoAnne with an E wiped the doll's open mouth with a rough, saturated brown paper towel. Even back then, it didn't seem like a very sanitary cleaning method to me.

As if it were slow motion, I could hear Janelle's reenactment of saving Annie. I heard the breaths; I heard the chest compression clicks. My heart was pounding even louder, and the entire classroom was shifting and rolling like the Scrambler at the St. Francis High School Carnival. Suddenly, I wasn't confident that my legs were going to continue to hold me up.

Janelle finished with Annie and skipped back to her seat. It was my turn. I stumbled forward, just close enough to grab the table for stability. Glancing over my shoulder, I realized to my horror that I was the last student to go. It was just me, creepy ass Annie, and JoAnne with an E.

"Next," she barked flatly as she eyed me.

I swallowed hard and heard my heartbeat pounding in my head.

"Next!" she repeated, gesturing for me to begin. I tried to speak, but my lips wouldn't move. I was completely panicking, melting down on the inside but frozen on the outside.

JoAnne with an E cocked her head to the side. "Hello? Let's move it along here. Ask Annie if she's okay," she prodded.

Paralyzed with terror, I stared blankly ahead, imagining my eyes empty and sightless, like Helen Keller in the made-for-TV movie, *The Miracle Worker*.

JoAnne with an E called out to my teacher with just the slightest hint of irritation. "Barbara? This last one's not participating in the exercise."

I was probably making JoAnne with an E very late for her commitment at the YWCA, setting up tables for canasta and Bloody Mary Social Hour.

I could tell my teacher, Barbara Cooksmyer, was writing on the overhead projector from the soft glow filling the room coupled with the squeak of Vis-à-Vis markers. The squeaking halted, and she snapped the projector off. Her clompy Danish clogs served as the vehicle bringing her ever closer to me with increasing volume.

My eyes focused on Annie's torso for the first time. She was wearing a red zip-up jacket with white piping, about two sizes too big for her. I was certain my grandpa had the same one in his closet at that very moment. My eyes traveled up to her face. *Her* eyes were closed and resting. She didn't look like she was in too much distress. She seemed more "okay" than me. I could see the holes in her head where the synthetic blonde hair plugs jutted out, a short mass of glossy tufts that fell back with the gravitational pull. Her nose had two open nostrils, and her jaw hung open, lips parted. Just like me, she wasn't moving or talking.

The memory of Annie's image haunted me for years. In the early stages of this book, I was fascinated to learn that Annie's face was modeled after the lifeless body of a young woman pulled out of the Seine River in Paris in the 1880s. A Jane Doe. She was dubbed *"l'Inconnue de la Seine"* or "the unknown woman of the Seine."

For the purpose of this book, I'll refer to her simply as *Annie*.

What happened to Annie? Neither Maddie, David, nor Robert Stack could have solved this one. Even Jessica Fletcher from Cabot Cove couldn't have made headway on this case for all the lobster in Maine.

There was no DNA testing back then, no cell phone tower location records, no surveillance video camera footage.

In a low-tech attempt to identify her body, Paris authorities displayed Annie in a street-facing window in the morgue. They hoped that *someone* would recognize her to claim the body and offer details about how she ended up in the Seine.

The face of Annie, which has been referred to as "the most kissed face of all time," holds secrets. She did at that time, back in Mrs. Cooksmyer's class, and she still does today. I didn't know it then, but many philosophers and historians wished, like Cher, that they could turn back time on Annie's timeless and evocative face—her countenance that became the impetus for a mannequin that would change the world with her life-giving education beyond the grave.

People crowded to see her, in hopes of identifying the "drowned Mona Lisa." Annie was like the head cheerleader and the public like her nerdy anonymous admirer with a big crush. The public couldn't solve her mystery, only get close enough for her magnetic pull to mesmerize and captivate them.

Back in the classroom, Mrs. Cooksmyer touched my shoulder. "Amy?" she asked sternly. "Why aren't you asking Annie if she's okay?"

Staring at Annie's face, all I could do was shake my head.

Barbara Cooksmyer put her face next to mine. I could smell the coffee and cigarettes on her breath. "Amy, just ask Annie if she's *okay*," she instructed in a firm voice.

"I, I—c-c-*can't*," I stammered. According to my mom, I used to have a pretty decent stutter when I was nervous.

"You're the only one who hasn't done it. Don't you want to *save* Annie?" demanded JoAnne with an E.

I forced myself to breathe deeply, but it did nothing to slow my heart rate. I tried again to answer. "No. I mean. Yes, but . . . *I can't*."

Scowling over the top of her glasses at me, Mrs. Cooksmyer demanded an explanation.

My mind was absolutely blank. "I, uh—don't know. I just can't." My cheeks felt as hot as two burners on a stove at the highest setting.

The whole class erupted in laughter.

Mrs. Cooksmyer waved her hand. "Pipe down, everyone!" she commanded.

She turned back to me, grabbed my shoulders, and turned my body to face hers. She lifted my chin to look at her. "I'm *very* disappointed in you," she seethed. I focused on the hand-drawn orange triangles that served as stunt doubles for her eyebrows.

I shook my head, broke my chin free from her hand, and dropped my eyes back to my Zips. "Sorry," I muttered.

"Well, you won't be receiving your official Red Cross CPR card with the rest of the class," she said in a condescending tone. I held back tears as I slunk back to my seat.

Mrs. Cooksmyer turned to JoAnne with an E. "I'm so sorry. I don't know what to tell you." She threw her hands up in frustration.

JoAnne with an E was pulling out an old suitcase from under the Formica table. I watched, transfixed, as she hoisted Annie into it unceremoniously. "Don't worry about it, Barbara," She shrugged. "There's an awkward one in every group."

chapter two

Criminals & Culprits

Guilty party associated with being responsible for a criminal offense

Clouds of breath puffed out before me just as I burst through them. I tore across the aggregate and leaned into the corner of my street like Tony Hawk on a skateboard.

"Tommy!" My shrill scream echoed into the night as I tried to catch my breath. I measured my strides as I approached the hedge in front of his house.

"Tommy! Open the door!" I shrieked as I hurdled over the hedge and fell straight into a pile of gravel. Pain seared through my knees as I rose, jagged pebbles sticking to the blood that began to pool on my skin. I threw myself onto the porch, and both my fists hit the door with a loud bang. Pounding on the door with all my might, I envisioned being grabbed by a bad guy from behind, so I started screaming louder.

Pounding harder, I gasped, "Tommy!" Tears streamed down my face.

There were many reasons for my panic—real and imagined. I truly did believe that a psycho carnie chased me into Tommy Boone's yard that night, but my brain was primed for this level of drama by many factors. Around this time in the 1980s, the US was experiencing a new crime wave the media was calling "child snatching." This was long before the days of Amber Alerts and national databases that track sex offenders. Eventually, in the '80s, we graduated to circulating police sketches advertising suspected perpetrators.

As a little girl, I remember staring, horrified, at the grainy black-and-white posters featuring these suspected perpetrators. It puzzled me that many looked very similar to the WWF wrestlers my great-grandmother watched—often with bandanas wrapped around their foreheads, and long stringy hair.

After the amateur police sketches came the milk carton kids. This was obviously before the internet, so apparently police work of that time included a shift or two spent standing over a huge photocopy machine while munching on a sprinkled donut and xeroxing flyers displaying missing children's information. As if their child were a cat or a ferret who had escaped. These flyers eventually graduated to a glossy printed version, actually printed on the back of milk cartons, the ubiquitous quart-sized containers that sat on practically every breakfast table in the country (back in the days when America drank cows' milk and had never actually heard of screw top containers of soy, almond, or oat milk).

Then the faces of the milk carton kids began appearing on other items, seeming, to my child's mind, like advertisements for kidnapping. Black-and-white photos of missing kids popped up on pizza boxes, junk mail envelopes, and eventually on grocery bags, displaying in bold, all caps their equally hair-raising and terrifying captions, "Missing," "Still Missing," and "Have You Seen Me?"

As an anxious, dramatic, imaginative kid, this was absolutely petrifying for me. I didn't *love* cleaning my room or picking up the dog poop every other afternoon the blazing hot sun, but it was obviously preferable to being snatched off the street to be brutally killed or sold into a sex slave ring. The way I saw it, kids were disappearing left and right. This caused a low-grade hysteria throughout the land. Kids I grew up with were pretty much convinced that if we were not with an adult, there was a good probability of being thrown into the back of an El Camino by bad guys.

I specifically remember terrifying myself while eating Honey Nut Cheerios at the kitchen table before school, reading the back of the milk cartons. Words like "last seen," "abducted," and "presumed" swam through my young mind as I ruminated over pictures of missing San Francisco Bay Area kids like Kevin Collins, Polly Klaas, and of course Adam Walsh, son of John Walsh of *America's Most Wanted*.

Even *The Berenstain Bears* made episodes about "stranger danger" for the first time. Parents were taking their kids to the police station to get them fingerprinted for the purposes of identifying them in case they should ever go missing. My parents actually role-played with us, each taking a turn pretending to be a shady-looking person in a kidnapper vehicle. My dad was semi-convincing as he pretended to need help finding his dog. Better still was my mom's stunning command performance posing as a creeper saying she knew our mom, who was in the hospital. So dark. Anyway, my "bad guy" mom tried to convince us she would give us a ride directly to see our mom if only we would hop in the *trunk* of a Pontiac Fiero.

This was when advocacy groups began to circulate the idea of picking a secret password that only you and your parents knew. What can I say? Secret passwords were trending. If, in fact, something happened to your parents, they would somehow be able to telepathically tell a safe person the secret password from their coma. Then instruct that person to come get you—brandishing the correct password of course.

Did my family have a secret word? Does the flag of the United States of America have fifty stars? Remember, my mom was all about safety, so, yes, **of course we did**. And, no, of course I won't reveal it. If I disclosed the password to you, it would be a coin toss as to who would kill me first, an actual murderer or my own mother. Safety first, my friends.

Annie was basically a milk carton kid of yore. She is timeless in her ambiguity, given that we can never know the truth of her life or her death. Pulled from the Seine with no visible marks or contusions, many assumed she took her own life. Due to her striking face and the shroud of curiosity around who she was, Annie quickly became the most popular Jane Doe in the morgue.

* * * * *

"Come down, money, come down!" yelled the carnie covered in grease who raised his arm above his head, yielding a wrench that rattled as he shook it.

The St. Francis High School Carnival happened every fall, and because those were the days of cash, the affluent student riders would lose the contents of their pockets if an attraction had an upside down or rocking component to it. As if on cue, immediately after he said it, cash began falling from the sky, floating to the earth below, followed by the pinging sound of a shower of coins.

Under the Ferris wheel, he threw his head back and laughed, full and robust, like Vincent Price on the track for the Haunted Mansion at Disneyland. His rat's nest of a ponytail bobbed up and down with the power of his voice. He lifted his head and a toothless grin spread across his face as he watched the mass of kids who staggered dizzily through the exit gate of the scrambler. His pupils were dilated, and he was definitely high as a kite, but that was totally lost on the elementary school version of me.

I watched him survey the crowd, scanning, scanning. I should have looked away faster, and a bolt of panic shot through me when our eyes locked. I gasped. Transfixed, I was terrified but couldn't help staring back.

He was what I pictured when I heard that heavy metal music, played backwards, said things like "Worship Satan." Church youth group camp had pretty much ensured we could never listen to a secular record again without assuming the artist was attempting to convert us to Satanism.

He outstretched his arm and pointed at me, motioning. "Come 'ere!"

What the—? I turned to my left and right then swung around to check behind me for another random elementary-school-age preteen. Or maybe he was pointing at Brody Jackson, who should be returning any second now from a bathroom break he had taken approximately seventeen hours ago. He'd been absent from the line for what I deemed to be a disturbingly long time. I looked behind me again. Come on, Brody! Pinch it off, will you! How long does it take?

"YOU!" shouted the carnie in a low, gravelly voice. Well, consider it confirmed: he was undoubtedly referring to me. *Ew.* Apprehensively, I moved forward with the Ferris wheel line, and as I inched closer, I could smell his greasy body. Repulsed, I immediately backed away, almost tripping over a mass of cords weakly affixed to the dusty ground by duct tape.

Why was I always noticed by the nasty guys? The old dudes, the disgusting ones like this. Not the *Bop* magazine guys of my dreams, like Rick(y) Schroeder from *Silver Spoons* and Kirk Cameron from *Growing Pains* or even one of the "Two Coreys" (Haim and Feldman). Instead, I was a creeper magnet, catching the attention of those who looked like registered sex offenders who had side hustles as carnies.

"Hey, wait!" he slurred, pulling a thin, rectangular bottle of brown liquid out of his back pocket. I continued my backward progression in the direction of the dunk tank. I wanted to turn and run but figured that would appear too obvious. I searched my mind for a solution. So I broke out in the robot, still walking backward. I figured that would throw him off. What kind of person would want to rape or murder someone doing an impromptu interpretive break dance?

Now, it was his turn to be creeped out. He started laughing at me, and I realized I was almost to the parking lot. I turned and bolted. I tore across the lot, through the field, and into Cuesta Park, which, I realized, was probably a poor choice of an escape route. The park was filled with excellent spaces in which to hide a dead body. It would suck so badly to be killed before my first prom, OR my birthday, which was coming up in a few days.

Back on the street, with my head full of evil, Satan-worshipping, cash-collecting, Jameson-drinking carnies chasing me, I realized I could make it to Tommy Boone's house if I just kept going for another minute. Sheer terror propelled me, and I soon arrived, panting and bloody-kneed on the doorstep.

Within a millisecond, before I could realize what was happening, the door flung open, and I did a half-pike tumble-to-stand across the threshold. The warmth of the house and the smell of chicken potpie hit me first. I couldn't remember ever feeling such relief.

Mr. Boone was standing behind the door, looking perplexed. "Uh, Amy Carlton?"

I was still catching my breath and realized then I was actually bleeding all over Tommy's dad's carpet. "Mr.—uh, Mr. Boone," I panted. "I'm—I'm so sorry. I just . . ." Suddenly I was embarrassed. Mortified. "Can I just—sorry—Can I please . . . Uh, can I please call my house?"

Calm but confused, he gave me a nod. "Let me get something for your knees."

I wanted to not care, but I cared. Still breathless, I looked down at bloodstains absorbing into the avocado-green shag carpet, and I watched tears roll off the tip of my nose.

My downcast eyes fell onto a pair of black Converse All Stars. Tommy.

"Ames, what are you doing?" He was holding an open package of Big-League Chew, and a massive pink bubble was protruding from his lips. By this time, my breathing had resumed a normal rhythm. I could hear Flock of Seagulls playing softly on the stereo.

"And I ra-a-an, I ran so far a-way-ay-ay."

He stretched out the hand holding the Big-League Chew. Misunderstanding, I slapped his calloused hand, thinking he was giving me a "low five," but he intended to give me a wad of gum, which only occurred to me when he shook the open pouch. When I connected these dots, my tears turned to giggles, and I wiped my eyes with the back of my hand.

Tommy brushed off the confusion as if he didn't even notice it. What a gift to be able to not overthink or read into a situation. "Ames, you wanna play *Frogger*? *Pitfall!*? Or—my brother just bought that new *Clue* game for the VCR. The same one you have." Tommy looked anxiously down at my bloody knees.

I closed my eyes and took a deep, grateful breath. "Yeah," I said. "Sure."

Just then, Mr. Boone reappeared with a first aid kit. I'm pretty sure it was purchased at the Montgomery Ward going-out-of-business sale of 1960. He held a bottle of nasty mystery liquid which I'm assuming was iodine, but to this day I'm unsure. He didn't have Band-Aids; instead, he cleaned my knees, slapped some mummy-like gauze on the wounds, and taped them up with some kind of yellowing athletic tape with basically zero adhesive.

The main problem, as I saw it, was that in just a few days, I was due to host my birthday party, which was to feature an actual reenactment of the whodunit movie *Clue* based on the popular board game. I had developed an entire script. I made copies and passed them out to the attendees, along with their character and suggested costume description. I was to be Miss Peach. (Who, by the way, was not a real character, at least not one from the original gang.)

The point is Pac-Man-colored vintage athletic tape was not going to work well with my Miss Peach color scheme. It included a peach dress, Maybelline Shimmering Shell lipstick, and my grandmother's mink. As I mulled over this conundrum, I studied Mr. Boone's kind face. He looked a bit weathered to me—let's get real, people, he was probably thirty-eight—but soft and approachable.

Another memory of Mr. Boone crossed my mind as I inspected the yellow athletic tape, and it wasn't as warm and fuzzy. Certainly not like my current experience with the makeshift first aid.

About a year prior, we had a school assembly about kidnapping. There had been reports of a white Econoline van casing the school and surrounding areas. (Why is it always a white van?) The school decided the answer was an assembly on "stranger danger" and the threat of kidnapping. Terrified, my walking-home-from-school partner, Jane, and I decided we might need a chaperone. An extra person to accompany us home, for safety's sake.

We were discussing this at great length in whispered tones during the class assembly when we both felt a tap on our shoulder from behind. Convinced it was a teacher or administrator about to give us a finger shaking, we slowly turned our necks to the side to glance behind us and face the tapper.

To our relief, it was just Wendi Romanoski. She had been wearing a bra since the third grade, and adolescence hadn't been very kind to her so far. I didn't know her very well, but I could tell she was a nice person.

"Hey," Wendi whispered, her braces shimmering in the dimmed multipurpose room light. "I live on Orange Grove."

There was a weird alleyway between our two neighborhoods, similar to the secret passageway from the conservatory to the lounge in the *Clue* board game. On one side of the fence, someone had spray-painted "Scorpions" with great care, even going to the lengths of using a stencil. It was impressive, and it stood the test of time as it remained there, becoming the hallmark of that alley for years.

Wendi leaned in closer. "I could walk a couple extra blocks with you guys." Her breath smelled like Doritos.

Jane and I turned to look at each other. Jane shrugged and nodded at me, and I nodded back. I turned back to face Wendi. "Okay," I said hurriedly under my breath. "Uh ... sounds good. Thanks, Wendi."

That afternoon, we set out for the journey home like the three musketeers. We chatted lightly, trying to distract ourselves from the eminent danger that could be lurking in a white Econoline van with blackout drapes and a suicide knob on the steering wheel. All three of us were nervous, trying not to bring it up. When we finally reached our street, we realized a massive flaw in our planning.

While Jane and I were overjoyed that we made it safely to our street, now we had no idea how to guarantee Wendi's safe arrival home on Orange Grove. As we were discussing this major foible, Mr. Boone drove by in his maroon Cutlass Sierra with the extended wheelbase. Tommy's towhead blond hair was just visible above the back window.

Mr. Boone pulled into his driveway and stepped out of the vehicle, carrying a black leather hard-sided briefcase, the kind with the combination lock on top. I presume this was for the safekeeping of, you know, very important confidential proprietary information from National Semiconductor where he worked on "audio amplifiers for wireless handsets," whatever that meant. His hair stuck up a bit on top from an eight-hour-old comb-over lacking enough Aqua Net to weather an entire day.

Tommy waved and dashed inside, blond hair bobbing up and down on his twelve-year-old head, yelling as he ran, "Off to do my paper route—gotta go!" I mean, he was a businessman, on the move. No time for fearing his potential fate in the back of a creepy van.

Mr. Boone strolled slowly, one hand in his polyester pants pocket, the other casually swinging his briefcase. Clearly overhearing our problem, he paused before reaching his porch.

"Do you ladies need a lift? I could run her a couple blocks over to Orange Grove," he called over the agapanthus.

Horrified by this offer, I winced at him and glanced at Jane. She had her lip curled and she was giving him a death stare. Clearly, she made the same assumption I did. The Cutlass Sierra was just a facade. He probably drove a white Econoline van at work, kidnapping kids on company time.

I shook my head at him. "No thanks, we're good," I called out flatly and turned back to face Wendi and Jane.

Wendi shook her head. Jane rolled her eyes and let out a woosh of air. *"Pssshh!"*

I couldn't believe I lived on the same street as this unsavory potential felon. Besides, who did he take us for, some dumb little girlie fools? I mean, fat chance, buddy. In fact, he should consider himself officially *on notice*. We had him in our crosshairs, *and* my mother (of course) was on the neighborhood watch committee.

After watching Mr. Boone shrug, turn, and walk into his house, unfortunately for Wendi, our best solution was to send her off alone.

We suggested she should just run home super-fast and hope for the best, which she did. Apparently, she made it, because she did show up at school the next day, un-kidnapped and all alive and everything.

* * * * *

The milk carton missing persons campaign lasted only a couple years. It is my understanding it was considered largely unsuccessful because the number of kids found alive was terribly low. Eventually, one doctor suggested that it was emotionally harmful for kids to start their day off eating breakfast cereal while reading about other, missing kids. I mean, he was *not* wrong. I'm living proof.

Arguably, the damage had already been done, resulting in a paranoid generation, haunted by the question "Have You Seen Me?"—and I, for one, am not over it.

Imagine Annie's family, searching for their missing daughter in the 1880s. If only they had milk carton kids back then, perhaps she wouldn't still be unknown. As it was, the urban legends picked up steam and branched off into a bunch of different story lines, even extending European borders, as some claimed she was German.

If Annie was murdered, perhaps it was by the company she kept. All kinds of nefarious characters could have been involved. Your basic "Professor Plum in the conservatory with the lead pipe" situation. If she indeed met with foul play, or associated with ill-intentioned folks, perhaps somebody from the underbelly world she hung around would have come forward . . . maybe even Zidler from the Moulin Rouge. If only.

When we're young, we often feel invincible. There are unsafe people all around us whom we often don't see as a threat. We assume nothing is going to happen to us. But as we have experiences and grow, we begin to develop intuition. Who is a threat? Who isn't a threat? It can be so hard to tell.

It often takes many turns around the *Clue* board to build a suitable accusation you feel comfortable making. Anyone who makes a snap judgment may have a chance of getting one—or maybe even two—elements in the "Confidential" file folder correct. But chances are, they are probably not going to have the murder, the weapon, AND the room all correct.

Decision making can be so difficult. Judging, particularly when wrong, can be so humbling. Cutting all safety tethers is almost always intensely unwise. So we try to walk that fine line as best we can, and it feels awkward, no matter which color *Clue* character you play.

chapter three

APBs & BOLOs

APBs (All-Points Bulletins) and BOLOs (Be on the Lookouts) are urgent announcements and updated notifications among police agencies containing details of an active situation

I'm hiding in the school library during lunch with my nose buried in a copy of *Are You There, God? It's Me, Margaret*, intermittently peeking above the cover to scan the room, wondering who was going to start singing first.

Crickets.

Just some sixth graders crowded around an *Encyclopedia Britannica*, and our ten-thousand-year-old librarian, Mrs. Tilly, with her horrifying hunchback, leaning over the squeaky book cart.

I eventually came to accept the fact that it wasn't going to be her to kick off the song.

There's a famous scene in *Ferris Bueller's Day Off* where John Hughes' film crew stumbles upon the Von Steuben Parade in downtown Chicago. Apparently, they slid their parade float right into the parade line on Dearborn Street in downtown Chicago. So there's Matthew Broderick as Ferris, up on the moving float alongside Danish girls in wooden shoes singing Wayne Newton's "Danke Schoen," and no one was the wiser.

By the following Saturday, the word was out that the crew would be in downtown Chicago a second time, to film the famous "Twist and Shout" part of the parade scene. Even without TMZ, the news got around, and thousands of people ended up flooding the area. They appear in the movie as extras—dancing and cheering during the song.

PS: If you haven't seen it, you're dead to me, and we can't be friends. Sorry not sorry.

Just like the Ferris Bueller parade scene, I waited, almost expectantly, for the monotony and the doldrums of normal life to be interrupted by an impromptu musical. At last, though utterly chagrined to admit it, I realized the kids at my elementary school weren't going to break out in random acts of song and dance. Nevertheless, my childhood remained one giant flash mob, if only in my head.

As I was just beginning the process of figuring out who I was, I simultaneously was watching '80s TV and movies and dabbling in what we shall call the *performing arts*. I loved putting on costumes, practicing voice inflection, and pretending I had Ferris Bueller's natural charisma. I made my imaginary performances on stage come to life with my flashlight-tied-to-a-bedpost spotlight and hairbrush microphone. I listened to the radio *all the time*. After school, I would lock myself in my room and switch the radio on. I would try to memorize the lyrics of all the new Top-40 songs so I could perform them in my bedroom to my audience of Cabbage Patch Kids.

My goals of onstage confidence were but dreams, assuaged only by practice and exposure, and trying again after some onstage catastrophes. Dance lessons were in full swing, and I figured that would be great practice for my onstage performance persona. Recital time rolled around, and my class was scheduled to perform two numbers in the recital, which was themed after some of the songs in a musical called *Leader of the Pack*. The first being a tap dance to the title song by the

Shangri-Las, as covered by Twisted Sister. The second number was called "Jivette Boogie Beat."

Props in dance recitals seemed to be all the rage at that time, and our dance teacher wanted each of us to personally craft a set of motorcycle handlebars for use in our first number and locate a poodle skirt to borrow or purchase from Goodwill for the second. The poodle skirt was easy enough, and my mom had the forethought to attach mine with Velcro, which was brilliant, due to the tight timeline we had for costume changes.

The handlebars were a different story. Of course, there were no YouTube videos back then. Essentially, we each had to pull a set of handmade motorcycle handlebars out of our asses, the only instructions given were to use a wire hanger from Lucky Dry Cleaners, bend it into the shape of a "V," and then wrap aluminum foil around it. I mean, *obviously*.

The dress rehearsal went fine. No issues, However, during the actual recital, various bloopers occurred. We made our debut onstage for the "Leader of the Pack" number two 8-counts too early, for starters. We found ourselves basically loitering out there on the stage, just hanging around staring at each other, shrugging, and swinging our handlebars around. Of course, Jill Kramer's handlebars nearly decapitated Michelle Castaneda by accidentally hooking onto her headband, which came detached, and so a headband-less Michelle spent the entire performance fuming and giving Jill the death stare.

Jill, on the other hand, had no idea what to do with her hands because she had no handlebars. (Because they got snared in Michelle's headband, gravity had its way with both items, and they crashed to the stage floor, being promptly swept up by security to prevent an accident.) Heather Ramsey had the choker for her next performance stuck to the backside of her costume for "Leader of the Pack," ensuring that she had a tail for the entire performance. Allison Kries was wearing her mother's pantyhose, about five sizes too large for her, and the ankles looked like elephant skin as the material pooled and drooped into her tap shoes.

I managed to escape the first number unscathed, but never you mind, I got mine during "Jivette Boogie Beat." After the nightmare of "Leader of the Pack," we tapped our way offstage, ready to change into our poodle skirts for "Jivette Boogie Beat." Our bags of costume changes were laid out behind a curtain just offstage. I remember ripping off my "Leader of the Pack" leotard, tossing it in the bag, flinging my handlebars like a boomerang into the abyss of umbilical cord–like knotted up-stage curtain ropes, and wiggling into my top and bobby socks. I grabbed my poodle skirt and slapped the Velcro together, slipped into my shoes, and lined up, waiting for our cue to make our stage entrance.

Everything was going along swimmingly until suddenly, right smack-dab in the middle of doing the *mashed potato*, I experienced a strange sensation, a looseness around the waist. Then, before my brain could register what was happening, I heard a rip and felt more looseness. I looked down to realize my skirt was actually coming apart. The Velcro was not secure enough to hold the heavy skirt, and it suddenly began to tear away. As it began its descent south of my hips, free-falling to the ground, I managed to grab it. I tried desperately to reattach it, to no avail. It was as if the Velcro had magically turned to butter. I stood, transfixed and clueless.

I could hear some uncomfortable shifting and muffled chuckles coming from the audience. Thankfully the spotlight was too bright for me to see the adults who were basically dying, trying to keep their laughter under control.

Looking back as an adult, I can honestly say it might've been more painful for the adults watching than it was for me. On one hand, it's a hilarious and unexpected catastrophe. On the other hand, you feel like you can't laugh because you know that's somebody's kid up there, on the verge of tears, dumbfounded and mortified.

I looked over to stage left and I could see my dance teacher looking at me, smiling and nodding, as if to say, *The show must go on!* She scrunched up her ballet skirt and held it with her fist while doing the choreography with one arm. This was her signal to me that I should just keep dancing with my skirt unattached and just hold it as best I could with the other hand. I mean, I guess the alternative was to run off the stage crying. The song was wrapping up, so I just grabbed the skirt with one hand, attempting to do the steps and one-armed motions with the free hand.

In the last few seconds of the song, we were supposed to each move into a preselected individual ending pose, making a V formation. I began to make my way toward my spot, still overwhelmed by the entire surprise of the skirt incident. I realized, much to my dismay, I could not, for the life of me, recall my final pose.

It was as if my mind were an Etch A Sketch and someone had shaken it clean—totally blank. Still clutching my skirt with one hand, I shot my other arm up with one pointed finger to the sky and lunged, pretending I was John Travolta in *Saturday Night Fever*.

At this point, the audience roared with laughter. The spotlight went off, the stage lights faded to black, and our class ran off the stage together.

I don't even remember making the decision to channel John Travolta during a 1950s sock hop dance; it was as if my brain were detached from my actual body. I was either mortally wounded by embarrassment or completely numb. I went home and I ate my emotions, whatever they were, in the form of a pint of chocolate ice cream, which seemed to be the appropriate clapback.

As I licked my wounds (and my spoon), I decided the real problem was I hadn't practiced enough in costume. I kicked myself for not managing to procure a copy of the "Jivette Boogie Beat" and practice more with the skirt on. But allow me to explain why that was next to impossible.

Let's say, for example, you like a certain song. You would like to have access to that song at any given time. In this day and age, that probably sounds like a simple process: log into iTunes, search for the song, purchase it, and commence to vibe out to your sick beats. Nay, young ones, this was not the simpleton's process of 1985. Lean in and listen to the trials and tribulations of how we had to get access to a song that we wanted to have in our possession.

First, you had to prepare to hunker down for an undetermined amount of time in front of your radio, procuring snacks, beverages, *Bop* and *Seventeen* magazines, whatever you could do to plant yourself and solidly commit to the long haul. Second, you had to cue up your cassette and tape recorder and position it gently by the radio speaker, and usually this step entailed simultaneously pressing the record and pause buttons, so that you were ready to go in case the melody of your favorite song began to make its way into your ears. Third: now keep in mind, your song could come on at any moment, but it could also take hours.

But you ran the risk of the song actually coming on while you were in the other room on the phone, particularly because it took approximately 934 years to make a phone call on a rotary dial phone. Should you experience a busy signal, you weren't on hold; you'd have to hang up and attempt the entire process all over again.

If the rotary phone conundrum didn't make you crazy, a disruption to your well-curated quiet recording space would. Inevitably, the song I was trying to record would come on, and as if on cue, my dad would walk into my room.

Like, ninety-five of the songs I recorded off the radio have my dad opening the door somewhere in the duration of that three-minute song. I'd be fist-pumping along to a scratchy, low-quality recording with a low hum or buzz in the background, suddenly interrupted by my dad's muffled voice saying something like, "Amy, have you seen my work gloves? I gotta move the wood pile," or "Amy, did you clean up the dog poop?" So, I mean, pick your poison; it was a gamble.

Alternatively, you could hit up your parents or a friend's older sibling to bum a ride to Tower Records and purchase a vinyl, professional copy of the song. This was all fine and good if you knew the artist and song title.

As for me, most of the time, I only knew the chorus. There was no app or "Ask Siri" to figure out the song. So, there I stood, like a complete moron, in the middle of Tower Records in a pink shorts romper and jelly shoes with a John Denver/Pete Rose haircut. I recall trying to ask for help from an employee by bashfully singing whatever melody or lyrics I could remember from "Let's Groove" by Earth, Wind & Fire. He was a shirtless guy with spiked black hair, wearing black lipstick, eyeliner, leather leggings, Doc Martens, and a dog collar with spikes.

I continued singing until I saw a look of recognition come into his eyes. He eventually nodded and said, "Follow me." I quit singing and happily skipped off behind him, in the wake of a combination of BO and leather. Never you mind! He was basically my hero.

Despite the flash mob in my head and numerous attempts to perform, I didn't love auditioning. Honestly, I probably had a measure of PTSD from the "Jivette Boogie Beat" poodle skirt incident. I discovered this when my friend Laurie and I decided to audition for the local community theater production of *Bye Bye Birdie*. For days, I practiced my chosen audition piece, "Brand New Life," which was the theme song from *Who's the Boss* starring Alyssa Milano and Tony Danza.

Laurie's mom drove us to the Los Altos elementary school where the auditions were to be held. I remember I had decided to wear my Jordache jeans and my mesh red "Tarzan top" that my mom had made for me—it was a wannabe Madonna outfit with its matching headband. I mean, come on. Who wouldn't give me the part on the spot? No need for callbacks.

We followed the sandwich board signs to classroom 211, and I could hear someone pounding on the ivories as we got closer. Laurie, ever the patriot, was planning on singing "You're a Grand Old Flag." She was in a red, white, and blue sailor suit and carried two batons with flags taped to the ends. I knew her plan was to march in place and twirl the batons while singing.

Suddenly, I started to worry that maybe my performance would be of lackluster value to the casting crew when compared to Laurie's Fourth of July parade-worthy routine. First, I failed to bring any props. It was like setting up the *Clue* game board and realizing you didn't have some of the weapons—like the candlestick and the wrench were missing. You sort of needed those items to make the game feel legit.

Second, I was not in a themed costume. I mean, I wasn't sure what kind of outfit would really accompany "Brand New Life" anyway, but I certainly didn't have anything, unless I wanted to wear a belted, silk one-piece romper or a power suit like Judith Light's stylist would have picked out for me. Like Miss Scarlet showing up in a yellow polka-dot bikini, it was definitely less convincing without at least an attempt at a costume.

I started to get a bit nervous. I bit my lip and looked down at my hands, which I was curiously wringing. Peeking into the door of the classroom, I could see it was packed. Like, can-of-sardines or bus-ride-accross-the-Mexican-border packed. It smelled like BO, bad breath, and sweaty genitals. Lying down on his side with one arm propping him up was a chubby, acne-covered, teenage gamer-type guy in a flannel shirt, jeans, and Adidas tennis shoes covered in various colors of paint. There was a Barbie Doll-type chick who looked incredibly bitchy, standing in the corner with her hands on her hips and a feather boa wrapped around her neck. She glared at the casting director, who looked exactly like Mr. Rogers, complete with the zip-up cardigan and the Keds sneakers.

"Thank you all for coming, once again," he said in a soft and gentle voice. "And if you haven't yet grabbed an audition number, please see Miss Rice in the back of the room and give her your sheet music for the accompanist."

Miss Rice was too old to be a "Miss" in my opinion. She was wearing a June Cleaver–type dress, but her body type was fighting the fit. She was the proud owner of a pair of jumbo-sized boobs threatening to burst her oval buttons, and a caboose in the back that meant business. Reading glasses were planted on top of her head, and her messy bun was falling loose into a thousand gangly gray tendrils.

She waved a clipboard and sing-songed the words *"Yoo hoo!"* at the sound of her name.

For some reason, that was it for me. I felt a wave of apprehension with a side of mild hysteria coursing through my body. Laurie made a beeline for Miss Rice through the throng of people. But I hung back at the doorway, gazing at my fingernails and listening to a couple of twin boys singing a duet of "Three Times a Lady" by the Commodores.

Suddenly, I couldn't imagine standing up there all alone, all eyes on me. I wanted to believe I had the confidence, but I was suddenly acutely aware that I didn't.

Panic shot through my body as Laurie enthusiastically traded her sheet music for a number and spun around, hopping back through the holes of folks as if she were playing hopscotch.

She held one hand on top of her head so her sailor cap wouldn't fall off as she bounced, and she clutched the batons in her other hand. "Well, Amy? Aren't you gonna go get a number?"

"Oh!" I said as if I hadn't heard a single word the casting director had uttered. "Um." I scrunched up my nose and shook my head. "Nah." I waved my hand at the room as if to say that those peons were beneath me. The truth was, I was scared shitless. At that point, you couldn't pay me to be in a kazoo choir, much less sing in front of those judgy people. Plus, who cared about *Bye Bye Birdie* anyway? It sounded like kind of a ridiculous play anyway.

Laurie's mom elbowed me, tilted her head to the side, and peered over the top of her Liz Claiborne sunglasses. "Oh, but you did all that practicing, and we're already here. Are you sure you don't want to just audition?" I shook my head and started bouncing my leg as if I were trying to squash a bug repeatedly.

Nope. Those people would never see me bust out my greatness—and it was their loss. They had created such a chaotic environment for auditioning that no way would I lower myself and my art to those standards. That's what I told myself, anyway.

The thing about acute anxiety is there is nothing on the planet at that moment that makes you feel like you're anything but hopelessly alone. It's like your body has betrayed you and suddenly you cannot feel the ground beneath your feet. As if someone unlatched a trapdoor underneath you and before you know it, you're free-falling and powerless to stop it.

I now know how empowering it is to receive a diagnosis. It's like landing on your feet after an impossibly long fall. Or maybe like Bo and Luke Duke in the General Lee, careening over a bridge under construction in Hazzard County on their way to meet up with Boss Hogg and Cletus at the Boar's Nest.

In my first couple years of sobriety, my psychiatrist brought up ADHD testing constantly. I scoffed at the notion, assuming he was crazy or probably got a bunch of cash or a trip to the Bahamas per ADHD diagnosis. I didn't have ADHD, for Pete's sake! I just had a super-busy life and some postpartum depression and anxiety. He was up to speed on my alcoholism and recovery. But I wouldn't give the ADHD suggestion any merit. Instead, I just continued to spin around on the merry-go-round of antidepressants, wondering why none of them seemed to "work" for me.

I left my psychiatrist's office after every visit with an armful of his non-optional printouts from medical journals, with titles like: "Women Diagnosed with ADD/ADHD during Midlife" or "ADHD and You: How Women Often Refuse to Accept a Diagnosis at First."

Finally, I was at my wit's end. I was on the top dose of an antidepressant that didn't seem to make a difference to me one way or another. I agreed at my very next visit to get tested for ADHD. Much to my surprise, I tested off the charts. I could tell my psychiatrist was trying very hard not to roll his eyes.

He remained professional, but he did smile and say, "I won't say I told you so . . ." as he handed me the test results. We both laughed.

I learned I was caught in a vicious cycle: My ADHD fueled my depression because I had always thought I was dumb, a slow learner, and that I wasn't dialed in to things like other people. I began to recognize that ADHD has probably helped me have amazing ideas, remember song lyrics, craft elaborate costumes and imaginary scenarios. But it also kept me jumping from one idea to the next, not really prepared for anything, and ready to flee the moment things became uncomfortable. My depression fueled my anxiety, because I was constantly afraid I wouldn't get all the details, or that I wasn't measuring up, or that I'd royally eff up.

Looking back on it now, I can see the strong coffee of that anxiety percolating as a child, even at that audition that never was. I was okay until I saw Laurie was wearing a themed outfit. What if that gave her a leg up (which it most certainly did, in my mind)? At that point, what other grave mistakes were possible?

Maybe I'd get distracted playing *Pitfall!* on the Atari and suddenly forget all the church kids had made a plan to meet up at the mall, hitting the Orange Julius at 14:00. Looking at my Swatch watch, I'd realize it was 14:48 and I was screwed. Even if I sprung it on my parents and demanded they take me, I'd never make it in time. Perhaps it would be some other fatally flawed, catastrophic mistake.

All of this equaled the bubbling cauldron of isolation. I thought I was just a kid who needed to get her shit together; I was secretly convinced I just had some weird issues and maybe everything could be explained by forgetfulness, excessive worry, and "a stubborn streak."

Standing back in the doorway of the audition classroom that day, my anxiety over the audition actually ended up cutting off my nose to spite my face. Laurie, not shockingly, made the callbacks for her unique, enthusiastic all-American routine. She ended up getting the part of Alice, the mayor's daughter in the Teen Chorus. You know what I got? Bupkis. That's what you get when you *refuse to audition*.

But I *always* wanted to feel a part of something, hence my desire to be a part of these musicals. I would let my anxiety swoop over me like a wave, and then if I turned my back, I'd fall over into the water and get electrocuted like David Addison in that *Moonlighting* episode, not realizing there was a TV in my hands.

If I could go back and have one single conversation with my childhood self, I would say, "Yes, it's going to feel uncomfortable, but if you push through that feeling and do it scared, it will be okay." And I mean that for *every* scary thing—not just the auditions, but also the

ADHD testing. Just be willing to let it feel uncomfortable . . . because the more you let it be uncomfortable, the more empowering it eventually becomes on the other side.

The thing was, I just couldn't bring myself to feel the terror and do it anyway. If I had auditioned, I'm sure I would have at least been given a pity role as a chorus member. Instead, because I had neither the knowledge or the language to understand or describe my condition, I hid behind my fear. I put up a defense mechanism at that audition. As if *they* were going to lose sleep for not recognizing this brilliant actor standing in the doorway of that hot, odorous classroom.

I just told myself they would never get the pleasure of being invited to the amazing cast party I had made up in my head with the greatest name on the planet: *The Tony ExtravaDANZA*.

Toward the end of *Ferris Bueller's Day Off*, after watching his father's Ferrari fly through the garage and into a ravine below, Cameron drowns emotionally after pretending to drown himself in the pool and being heroically saved by Ferris.

Coming out of his comatose state after Ferris attempts to revive him, Cameron jokes to Ferris, "Ferris Bueller, you're my hero."

Which is, in a meta sense, true because Ferris is who we all essentially wanted to be. Someone who life just kind of "works out" for, despite our shortcomings. Someone who could just seize a day here and there, just for fun and good measure. Someone who could slyly sneak a parade float onto a Chicago street and get away with joining Dutch girls in singing "Danke Schoen" with, of course, an ever popular and obvious smooth transition into "Twist and Shout."

As much as I wanted to play the role of Maddie Hayes from *Moonlighting*, formerly known as the "Blue Moon Shampoo" girl, it inevitably worked out that I was awkward. I eventually started to grow into my quirkiness, learning to use my unique talents for some pretty epic prank phone calls, thank you very much. I discovered how to improvise and think on my feet when my imagined leading lady role didn't work out. Or my skirt fell off. In the end, all these performances remind me that sometimes to reach a goal, you must push through the fear. Confront when necessary. Do it scared.

If the mysterious drowned girl, Annie, in 1880s Paris was indeed the victim of a violent attack, perhaps nobody ever gave her the crucial advice to never let yourself be taken to a second location. There would be no clue as to her last known whereabouts, no APB out for her attacker, no security camera footage for the police to review. Even if you're scared, you must fight that fear to save your life. You have to use all your tools: your voice, your hands, your knees. Don't you dare forget the candlestick, the lead pipe, the knife, the revolver, the rope, and the wrench.

The more common ailments of today are also scary: anxiety, trauma, untreated mental illness, even though there are solutions for these conditions nowadays. But that soul-gripping fear can be enough to freeze you in your tracks and separate you from a solution. But if you freeze, chances are the outcome won't be good: you could be attacked, snatched, become a prisoner of your own mental conditions... or you could find yourself drowning at the bottom of the Seine.

But to be physically pursued and attacked? I mean, that is fright in its most primal form. It's the stuff nightmares are made of. And if *Annie* were chased, pushed, thrown, or otherwise terrorized into the Seine against her will that night, then her final moments on earth were spent proverbially drowning in debilitating fear... and then literally drowning in the overwhelming water.

But there will be a second act to this play: her eventual rebirth would be so grand, so random and astoundingly awkward, it was the surprise "Twist and Shout" that no one saw coming.

chapter four

Badge Bunnies & Holster Sniffers

Slang for a certain type of individual whose personal appearance and behavior is aimed toward attracting a police officer

I watched as Miranda Chase added another layer of blue mascara. She and I were getting ready for the eighth-grade dance, both wearing blue Hawaiian shirts. Mine had flamingos on it; hers had a hibiscus flower. We teased our bangs, taking turns holding the blow-dryer vent brush up while we sprayed Aqua Net hairspray with the other hand. Then of course, we added our charm bracelets that we had purchased for five dollars at the De Anza Flea Market. We knew we looked amazing.

Off to the dance we went, in the back of Miranda's mom's "Bahama Blue"–colored Ford Aerostar van. She dropped us off, and we walked in just as "Love Shack" was starting up. The same DJ was there every month. It appeared this was a regular gig for him, and sure enough, there he was, perched behind the booth, one hand on his ear, the other hand spinning a record. His chocolate-colored David Lee Roth perm was bouncing in time as he jutted his chin forward and retracted it, nodding fiercely to the beat. The lights were low, and a bunch of side ponytails and Max Headroom haircuts were bopping around to The B-52's. The signature '80s junior high school scent (a custom blend of Drakkar Noir and Exclamation perfume) instantly went to our heads. Miranda and I looked at each other and began to giggle.

Month after month, the DJ's outfit was consistently entertaining and eyebrow raising. This month was no exception, and it did not disappoint. Tiny Richard Simmons-like striped dolphin shorts overtly cupped his balls and butt cheeks. He wore a neon yellow tank top from "The Mystery Spot" in Santa Cruz. Now, let me just tell you that I had never before seen a man with so much hair. Hair was bursting out from his neck, springing from his back, arms, and chest like a Chia pet. It spilled off his skin in a thick mass, as if perhaps he were the love child of a sasquatch and Michael J. Fox in *Teen Wolf*.

I'm forty-five years old now, and I still struggle with having no filter. But back then? Fuhgeddaboudit. I don't think I knew what being socially appropriate was, though I could have probably learned if I looked closely at the reactions of some of my fellow churchgoers after I opened my mouth.

At any rate, I said in a rather loud voice to speak over the music, "I wonder if the DJ perms his *pubes*."

Miranda, who had an organically loud voice, turned to look at me and scowled, not understanding. *"What?"* she said, cupping her hand around an ear.

I leaned in toward her and repeated myself, a little louder.

She cocked her head to the side and furrowed her brow. "Huh?" Her loud voice effortlessly projected over the song's chorus.

I cupped my hands around my mouth and leaned forward to put them against her ear to communicate, but she pulled away and shook her head. Turning her face toward mine, she pointed to her

Maybelline Shimmering Shell–lipsticked lips and tapped her pointer finger on her chin.

"Need to see your mouth when you talk!" she instructed.

With all the breath and volume I could muster up, I screamed as loud as I could, "I wonder if he perms his PUBES!"

I should have been paying closer attention to the song.

I happened to scream "his pubes" at the point in "Love Shack" right after Fred Schneider says, "You're *what*?" when there are about thirty seconds left in the song. Normally, there are about two full beats of silence after "You're *what*?" Tragically, that was not the case this time. The entire junior high multipurpose room got the shock of their young lives when they heard:

Fred Schneider, in "Love Shack": *"You're what?"*

Amy Carlton, screaming: *"HIS PUBES!"*

Kate Pierson, in "Love Shack": *"Ti-i-i-i-n roof . . . rusted."*

Approximately 993,205 of my classmates froze, heads turned in my direction. A few gasps popcorned through the air.

I scanned the room in what seemed like slow motion as I tried to process what just happened. I felt like all the air left my lungs, like I had been kicked in the stomach. My knees felt like they would buckle, and my face flushed and probably turned the approximate color of Prince's *Purple Rain* coat.

My entire junior high school heard me scream "pubes." It was the awkward bush reference heard round the world. It would be a fair few months before I braved showing up at the junior high dance again, and I *may* have dubbed a disguise following this incident and remained, for the rest of my time in junior high school, slightly incognito. It cannot be confirmed or denied.

Despite this mortifying happenstance, dancing went on to become my first workout experience . . . safe at home, lest the public be inadvertently exposed again to my "PUBES" battle cry or think I had developed a sudden onset case of Tourette's syndrome. I already had enough issues of my own, thank you very much. Hard pass. I had no interest in becoming a repeat offender. But I did have all the home accoutrements (jump rope, weights, stopwatch, etc.) to the "Get in Shape, Girl!" exercise gear that spotlighted on rhythmic ribbon dancing.

I then graduated to Alyssa Milano's (star of TV's *Who's the Boss*, duh) at-home workout video called *Teen Steam*—which, I might add, contains an epic mid-workout freestyle rap, performed by Alyssa and her two workout buddies.

I felt betrayed by my body. At the exact onset of puberty, my hips began to expand at an alarming rate, eventually taking on their own persona. Try as I might, I could not escape my pear shape; it followed me around like a lost dog, as it does today. Not understanding there really wasn't much I could do about that predicament, I decided I needed to take charge and step it up.

Like many girls, my obsession with exercise and food started long before I became an adult. It started out when I overheard someone saying they could sense a difference between holding my hand and my neighbors' hand, which was "much thinner." I remember thinking there was something about the word "thin" that was not right. It was just another area where I was apparently falling short. Over time, I collected a variety of similar experiences that led me to become obsessed with exercise as a young teen.

Next came the fat-free era. Fat-free pizza that tasted like cardboard with a sprinkle of cheese and a dollop of freezer-burned marinara sauce. Fat-free cookies that tasted like chocolate air. Even restaurants participated in the fat-free movement, providing a section on the last page of their menu called "guiltless." Eventually, a YMCA opened near my house. I knew a few people at school who had procured memberships with a student discount, and so I thought, screw it, why not give it a whirl?

It was a special time in workout fashion. I would be doing you a disservice if I failed to examine some of the details here for you. The '80s were technically over, so legwarmers had been replaced by "slouchy socks" that we pulled up to our kneecaps and pushed back down over our calf, basically creating three poufy "donuts" on top of our ankles.

The mesh tank tops and mono-boob sports bras of the Jazzercise era weren't going out of style, but new fads were coming in with the 1990s in addition to the slouchy socks. Enter the thong leotard. Now, for some reason, owning a thong workout leotard preceded owning thong underwear, at least for myself and my friends. This resulted in a bunch of girls all wearing thong leotards over their bike shorts, with visible panty lines. The thongs actually drew *more* attention to our underwear. The effect was butt cheeks looking like a 3D relief map, bisected by the thong not unlike the I-5 freeway from the Bay Area to LA, surrounded on either side by lumpy topography.

The cheap rates at the YMCA offered a spectrum of customers across all walks of life. I'll never forget Roger, a wire-framed-Coke-bottle-glasses-wearing beer-bellied man in his sixties. He was honestly probably about forty, but who could tell at age thirteen? Everyone looked ancient. Roger wore the same thing *every single time* I saw him, in each and every class. His uniform of choice was a super high-cut pair of maroon cotton running shorts with white piping. He wore a white crew neck Fruit of the Loom shirt tucked in tight over his belly. The cherry on top of Roger's signature look were the accessories: a terry cloth maroon sweatband on his head that matched his shorts, burgundy Reebok trainers, and gray terry cloth wristbands. What can I say? He was an accessory guy!

Every time he saw me, he would say, "Carlton? Where are you going to go to college?" We'd had this conversation so many times before, and I knew he had gone to the University of Redlands.

"Redlands," I would answer, smiling and rolling my eyes. He had a nervous energy and kind of this tic-like behavior that he did to prepare for each class. He would jump up onto the step and squat, then jog in place on top of the step. Then he would stop and hold a squat for twenty seconds or so. The whole time, bending his arms at the elbow and making fists, rapidly moving them back and forth obsessively as if there were a punching bag in front of him.

My step was usually somewhere in his vicinity. I could always tell when he was doing that weird warmup move because he moved his arms so fast it created a breeze, and he huffed and puffed audibly. I was pretty sure other people avoided him, but I thought it was fine if he had a couple of screws loose. Sidebar: Back in those days, we never thought that anybody had ADHD, or autism, or anything like that. Nobody really understood neurodiversity; we just knew that one "quirky guy" in the low-impact step aerobics class at 4:45 p.m. on Tuesdays and Thursdays at the Mountain View YMCA, that quirky guy was Roger.

Eventually, it became harder to get into classes as the local popularity of the YMCA grew. It wasn't long before the women's locker room reflected the uptick in memberships, as evidenced by the increase of older naked grandmas with gross low-hanging boobs.

There was one lady who fascinated me. She had short black hair and this whole routine. She would do tai chi in the sauna then take a shower in her shower shoes. After her shower, she would take out a small travel-sized Buddha statue and set it on the countertop in front of the mirror, placing an orange in its lap. The final phase of her ritual included planting herself in front of the mirror, in the nude, and blow-drying her crotch.

Between the crowded locker room, Roger, and the crotch blow-drying lady, I decided maybe I was going to switch back to the home video workouts for a while. Which I did.

My mom had a VHS tape called *Sweatin' to the Oldies*, with Richard Simmons. During those times, Richard Simmons had a cable TV show on the public access channel where he would guide senior citizens in this routine called *Sit and Be Fit* (or maybe it was the era of *Silver Sneakers*, I can't remember which). I loved that video so much that it actually broke inside our Hitachi VCR with the pop-up tape insertion mechanism.

I started to notice around this time how much effort it took to look presentable. None of my clothes fit right anymore, and I wondered how it was that some of these girls look so effortless at school with the way that they dressed. These were the popular girls, the crowd I was not a part of. A different level of society. These were the girls who seemingly woke up with their blue mascara already applied, their bangs already teased, and their perms already set with product. Whatever look they were going for, whether it was the Pat Benatar, the Jessica McClintock, the United Colors of Benetton, or the Annie Lennox, they truly made it look easy.

There's a term my friend and I coined for this species: they are the *down girls*. You know, they are just down for anything. Wanna roll to the beach after school? They have a swimsuit in their backpack! *They're down!* Meet up at the Mountain View Library for a study sesh? They just happen to have their fake "teacher's pet" glasses from Claire's accessories. *They're down!* Or maybe just a casual trip to the strip mall on Grant Road and El Camino to swing into Sally Beauty Supply for a new crimping iron. They have their hair pulled back into a banana clip with romantic whips floating around their faces… *plus*, they have their mothers' credit cards and notes giving permission to use them. *They're* so *down!*

Me? I woke up at 6:00 a.m., showered, slapped on Maybelline foundation in a sad attempt to cover my zits. Then, to deter anyone from looking too closely at my face, I applied approximately thirty-two coats of colored mascara. Then I'd start the marathon of blow-drying my perm with the diffuser and Salon Selectives scrunch spray, ending of course with the vent brush, teasing comb, curling iron, and Aqua Net. Going through the whole routine of teasing the bangs, spraying, hitting it with the blow dryer, then the curling iron, more Aqua Net, vent brush to fluff it out and up. More Aqua Net. And of course, finish off with a final hit of the blow-dryer. By the time I was done, I was ready for bed again.

Eventually I would just call it done, giving myself an "A" for effort. I knew I had done the best I could with what I was given. Inwardly, I felt like a cross between Bette Midler and Rodney Dangerfield. Or like Liberace and Barbara Streisand had a baby out of wedlock. *Desperately Seeking Susan* wasn't nearly as desperate as I was trying to find an outfit each day.

I stepped it up to another level, one day rifling through the VHS collection again, only to find my mom was a true G and purchased the latest Jane Fonda workout video. I could not believe how amazing Fonda looked working out in her liquid leather glittery blue leotard and metallic tights. I wondered if she ever broke a sweat for real. Her hair bounced perfectly and stayed in that feathered look. I just didn't understand how people did that. Jane, obviously, was the original *down girl*.

I mean, let's get real here. This is a great equalizer: We've all had our unfortunate seasons of looks. Me, with my thong leotards over visible panty lines, and Annie, whose second act look is basically the female version of *Weekend at Bernie's*. But she wasn't always so awkward.

The Annie of Paris in the 1880s was young, attractive, and captivating. The pathologist at the Parisian morgue was fascinated by her.

Nobody knows how many other dead people he was attracted to, but Annie was his favorite. So much so that he had a plaster cast made of her face to preserve it before she was buried in a pauper's grave. Make of that what you will.

The fascinating and slightly whimsical countenance and striking features of Annie's gentle face inspired many reproductions of the death mask. Eventually, these copies of her face became the "lava lamp" of their time, appearing in stylish homes all over Paris. Annie's expression popped up in the surrounding shops and crafters' booths in the Beaux Arts Village, in the shadow of the Sacre Coeur. Poets, writers, philosophers, and aristocrats all over Europe rushed to purchase one, as if the mask was the last Cabbage Patch Doll at Toys "R" Us on Christmas Eve 1983.

Annie's delicate face provided mystery and intrigue in the bohemian circles of Paris for generations. And then, the mask went off the grid, so to speak. As fads do, the mask of Annie took the back burner to something else; perhaps another piece of plaster countenance was trending. Ahem—boobs. Whatever the reason, Annie's trail went cold. On hiatus from the spotlight of popularity as fashion decor trends came and went. Until this case took a wild and unexpected left turn.

chapter five

Interviews & Interrogations

Eliciting information and gathering facts germane to the case

I screeched into the high school parking lot, driving the Chevrolet Cavalier station wagon I inherited from my grandfather and had prematurely pimped out before my sixteenth birthday. It had fuzzy dice for the rearview mirror, a strawberry air freshener in the shape of a pine tree, a Jesus fish on the hatchback (I mean, obviously), and a Case Logic visor CD organizer. The crowning jewel, my prized possession, was an upgrade to the stock radio. It was a Pioneer cassette/CD combo radio with the orange illuminated background.

I lowered the radio volume to avoid a Ren-in-*Footloose*-when-he-gets-pulled-over-for-blasting-loud-music scenario.

"*Everybody's workin' for the weekend!*
Everybody needs a new romance . . ."

I was not an experienced driver. I had taken exactly *one* driver's ed class but of course insisted that I could (and should) practice driving. I had convinced my mom to let me drive to school that morning. Without question, it was an absolutely harrowing ride.

I pulled up into the drop-off lane, jammed on the brakes, and basically gave my mom and myself whiplash as I jerked us to a stop. Then I dislodged the stereo from its housing and pulled it out by the handle.

I grabbed my backpack from the backseat and eased it onto one shoulder, as we did. "Bye, Mom!" I slid out of the driver's side.

My mother, who hadn't yet detached her white knuckles from the dashboard, grunted through the Helen Keller stare. I headed in the general direction of my locker, swinging the stereo-on-a-handle as if it were a lunchbox full of Hot Dog on a Stick in my left hand.

In my right hand, I brandished about thirty-eight keychains from Claire's Boutique. They included a Koosh ball, a miniature underwater aquarium ring toss game, a boom box made of Pez, a miniature lightbox with a picture of my youth group at Great America, and a Rubik's Cube. The jumbo-sized keychain contained a mere THREE *actual* keys: one for the Cavalier door, one for the ignition, and one house key. Barely enough to necessitate ONE keychain, let alone thirty-eight-ish keychains . . . which, in my hand, were about the same weight as a Costco pot roast, or a small newborn, your choice.

According to my schedule, printed on a dot-matrix printer, I was placed in "Math A" class, affectionately known in my circle as "Bonehead Math." This nickname wasn't a surprise to me, but the casual manner in which the class was conducted was. Our teacher was a sweet, laid-back middle-aged woman named Mrs. Glyer. The most amazing thing about Mrs. Glyer was her "uniform." Every day, she wore graphic T-shirts tucked into business dress slacks, with wool socks and clogs. Her look also included wire-framed glasses and a fuzzy halo of permed brown hair, the classic '80s white woman Afro—both a bit dated at that point. You do you, Mrs. Glyer, work it.

Anyway, Mrs. Glyer broke the class into quadrants, randomly selected, and instructed us to introduce ourselves to the others in our groups. She asked us to share something unusual from our lives that was particularly out of the ordinary. I looked at the other participants in my cohort as we slumped into our desks with the fake wood laminate. Never was there a more lackadaisical, apathetic group of math students. Ever.

My desk featured an artful carving of the band name "Megadeth." I heaved a heavy sigh and wondered if the carver had passed "Math A" and gone on to bigger and brighter things. Perhaps the carver was now working on a Pixar animated film, or on a design team. More likely, he or she was probably living in the garage of their parents' multimillion-dollar 1950s Silicon Valley home, playing Nintendo 64 and eating day-old Domino's Pizza crusts. Oh, dear God. I closed my eyes and privately held a moment of silence for my future.

The first kid in my quadrant was a girl named "Rouqil" (pronounced "Row-keel"), which, she was quick to point out, was "liquor" spelled backward. She told us her mother made up that name because she was heavily drinking the night Rouqil was conceived. I remember trying *very hard* to maintain zero expression on my face as I nodded understandingly. That may have been a bit of an overshare for Rouqil, but what's a little too much information between quadrant-mates?

Next there was Ashley Davis—a boy named Ashley. At the time, that was primarily a girls' name, except in historical fiction romance novels, as far as I could tell. He was a cute, blond preppy kid with the kind of "Flock of Seagulls" hair on top and a fade on the sides and down the back. And he was a sharp dresser. He wore V-neck sweaters from the Gap and pressed khakis, and he carried a messenger bag while the rest of us still had standard-issue Jansports. He was fairly quiet—not shy, per se, but one of those types who wasn't going to waste a bunch of time making meaningless chitchat. Anyway, Ashley told us he had just moved to California from Rhode Island, which was, for us, like another country.

Sidenote: That was the only year Ashley was preppy. By junior year, he had a full-blown leather moto ensemble going on, including assless chaps (over his jeans, of course!) and a shiny Ducati motorcycle. He also took up smoking and spoke even less than he had as a freshman. As you were.

Finally, there was Renata. She was from Guatemala—an exchange student who constantly drew pictures of miniature horses in various tiny scenes on her canvas binder. A horse in a pasture; a horse at the mall; a horse wearing pants; a horse in a Santa Hat drawing a carriage through the snow at Christmastime; a centaur in outer space. Renata spoke only Spanish, which pretty much left Rouqil and me as the potential spokespeople for the group. There was no way I was going to vie for power against the product of an intoxicated impregnated mother, so I bowed out of the spotlight and let Rouqil take the floor.

When Mrs. Glyer instructed us to come up with a team name for our group, the four of us just stared at each other. I awkwardly messed around with my mechanical pencil, pretending it was out of lead. Ashley picked at a thread hanging off his messenger bag. Rouqil took out her Dr. Pepper–flavored Bonne Bell Lip Smacker and began to apply another coat. Renata commenced a new horse drawing with one of those fat ballpoint pens that had sixty-five different color options at the click of a turning mechanism.

The volume around us rose as the other students began to brainstorm their team names. Laughter and shouts rang out as they all discussed and voted on different name options. Our quadrant just sat there in clumsy silence, like a B-movie version of *The Breakfast Club*.

Finally, Rouqil asked, "Do you guys have any ideas?"

Ashley shook his head without looking up from the stitching that was apparently so riveting.

Renata shrugged her shoulders and replied, *"No se."*

Rouqil turned her attention to me.

"Nope," I said. The truth was, I could have come up with something, but I was afraid. What if I threw an idea out there and everybody made fun of it? I just decided it was safer to be a complete parasite and mooch an idea off someone else more qualified to handle this task.

Mrs. Glyer began making the rounds, going from table group to table group, asking for team names and walking back to the chalkboard to write them down. There were "The Flintstones," "The 49ers," "The Purple People Eaters" and "Contagious Corn." (Still wondering about that one—OR maybe my memory is bad, and it was Contagious *Porn*? In either case, WTF?)

Inevitably, she clogged her way over to our group. "And what's your team's name going to be here?" Mrs. Glyer asked in her cheerful, effervescent voice. Her request was met with four blank stares.

"Oh, come on, you guys. What's your name going to be? You have to come up with something." I squirmed in my seat as boy Ashley managed a fake cough attack.

It was Rouqil who broke the ice and saved us. She cleared her throat and said, "We Don't Give a Shit."

Mrs. Glyer stood there for a few long seconds with her hand cupped to her ear, blinking. Then she began slowly nodding. "Okaaaay," she said kindly and affirmingly. "That works."

She spun on her clogs and clip-clopped over to the chalkboard. She tapped out "WE DON'T GIVE A SHIT" in a cloud of yellow chalk dust.

For the entire school year, that was our team's name. Somewhere around Veteran's Day, the name was abbreviated, shortened to "WDGAS." This was because (a) the entire sentence was too lengthy to write on group assignments, and (b) the principal was making his rotations through the classrooms, observing all the teachers in late fall. No one wants to be caught letting students use an expletive as their team's name in the classroom, am I right?

The moral of the story is: Being in "Bonehead Math" has affected me exactly *never*. Except for *the people*, who made a fantastic memory in the treasure trove of my youth.

PSA: Unsolicited advice for the high school students—don't be defined by your SAT scores, your math class, or any of that BS. Later in life, *you* will not give a shit.

High school is so interesting. And awkward.

There's a scene in *Sixteen Candles* where Molly Ringwald walks onto the bus, on her forgotten birthday, takes one look at the chaos on wheels, and says, "I *loathe* the bus."

I felt that way about high school in general. But one of life's coping skills is finding those habits and connections that get us through the day, particularly in otherwise unpleasant situations. In every class, I'd observe the other students, watching for that one kid who was stifling giggles over the same dumb things that I was. By doing that, I'd find my person in each class.

Navigating those early high school years was especially interesting as I was exposed to entirely new kinds of people—beginning with Rouqil and Renata. I was literally raised in the epitome of a white suburban bubble. The only hairline cracks of diversity in my primary school were a small percentage of Asian kids. Mountain View High School, however, had city buses dropping off loads of kids every morning from the Air Force base on the other side of El Camino. For the first time, I was exposed to people who weren't exactly like me.

Speaking of buses: here in Washington, the state provides school bus transportation. In fact, if you are following behind a bus here, you'll notice they stop approximately every three feet to pick up kids. No hoofing it for blocks and blocks to the nearest stop like you see on the movies. Nope. The buses here, at least in our neighborhood, pretty much pick kids up at their doorstep. It's more like a chauffeuring service.

School buses were not really a *thing* in California growing up. We would take one on a field trip here and there, but they were not used for daily transportation. Enter the city bus, the one that the kids from the other side of El Camino used. My friend Jane and I had a brief experience taking them. *Somehow*, our mothers were tipped off that there was a city bus stop at the end of our street. Probably some "nosy Nancy" type other mother who ran into them at Safeway let them know that the bus line on Miramonte would take us straight to the stop near the "grassy knoll" at the high school, which was essentially the Grand Central Station for minors who commuted to school.

I mean, look. As a parent myself, I get it. If you had the opportunity, would you rather pop your perfectly capable high school student on the city bus every morning or stumble around in your bathrobe with only ONE coffee in your system, frantically searching for your glasses and a bra so you wouldn't be completely indisposed, because you KNOW you'll run into the ever-chatty dean of students right there in the drop-off line, who will ask what your thoughts are on "Measure A" coming up on the ballot in November? Caught totally off guard, you pull some BS out of your ass and are eventually saved by the parade of honking braless mothers in *their* cars behind you, spilling out onto the street. By the time you get home, the percolator has shut off, gifting you a three-quarters-full pot of lukewarm coffee, and you've missed half of *Good Morning America*.

Seems like an easy choice to me.

Eventually, a gang fight broke out on the bus, and Jane's mom and mine both decided to take pity on us and remove us from our bus kid status. Save for a brief bike riding stint (until I ran over a squirrel), they ended up caving in and just splitting up the carpool driving obligations. We got lucky.

Mountain View High School was a great equalizer of teenage kind, providing me with an education on many levels. There were clubs with names like "Mexican American Hermanos," and the school had a Black Student Union. I was fascinated and sometimes confused by my fellow students. For example, groups of boys roamed the halls, proudly sporting Bulls or Raiders Starter jackets *without cutting off the tags*. Were they planning to return the jacket later if the team hit a losing streak? I'd ponder these questions while sipping my cherry New York Seltzer at lunchtime.

Always an amateur sleuth, I also started investigating why some students got a "free" lunch every day from the cafeteria while everyone else had to pay $3.50. I was shocked to discover they qualified for subsidized meals because their parents were struggling financially. This was an eye-opener. As was Rouqil's distress when she went to pull out her math book on a Monday, only to realize she left it at her dad's girlfriend's place over the weekend. At first, I gave her the side-eye, thinking she was irresponsible.

Then I put myself in her shoes. I forgot things all the time. Rouqil had been so focused on trying to spend time with her dad, who she had not seen in two years, she forgot to wrangle her own stuff. None of the adults in her life pitched in to remind her to grab her math book. My mom, ever the Girl Scout leader, was an excellent marksman when it came to having everything you needed and reminding me to do the same. She hit the bull's-eye every time.

Even Ashley, a future *Grease II* "cool rider," was a real live latchkey kid! He was on his own after school since his mom worked doubles. I had only seen latchkey kids on after school specials. Or so I thought. It suddenly occurred to me that I, too, went home to an empty house a couple of times a week, while my mom was off getting her master's degree. And by the way, guess how my mom got to San Jose State so she could use the drive time for studying? That's right, people: she took the city bus.

And so it was that high school was a turning point, my first realization that there was a world out there that grew up differently, thought differently, acted differently. Experienced life differently. Not everyone had thirty-eight keychains, a free hand-me-down car from their grandpa with a fancy car stereo upgrade, and a visor full of CDs.

In the movie *Overboard*, there's another Annie character. *Overboard*'s Annie is a snobby rich bitch, and she's just about as clueless as I was (still am) about privilege. Only after she falls off her yacht into the water, assisted by her subsequent case of amnesia, does she get a dose of reality knocked into her. *Overboard*'s Annie had all the physical luxuries and privileges she could ever want; she was eventually found, but after getting a taste of the simple life and its hidden treasures, she realized she'd prefer to be lost, and she ended up with the best of both worlds.

Neither she nor her hunky costar and real-life partner, Kurt Russell, realized she had it in her to be kind, grateful, and open-minded. But it took a turning point for her to be placed in a position where she could see and attach to some intangible truths. She allowed herself to change and grow, instead of staying stagnant.

My friend Jane and I were allowed to get a city bus "exemption" because of a *safety issue*. We were lucky enough to have an alternative means of transportation to get to and from school, since our mothers didn't work outside the home. Our families had the luxury of making alternative arrangements. By default, that concept proposed the idea that the same safety issue that *wasn't* okay for us apparently *was* okay for other bus riders who had fewer choices. Like discovering in health class that Pixie Stix were basically powdered diabetes in straw form, these concepts were all new to me.

We don't have a clue about Paris Annie's background. But we do know she wasn't found in the safest part of town. She was placed in the window of the morgue, front and center, in hopes that someone from the Parisian public could identify her. It seems that even then, a missing white woman tended to get a heavy load of media and police attention and assistance.

Solving a missing white woman's case usually becomes top priority. A media blast goes out to the Blue Moon Detective Agency, Jessica Fletcher, Columbo, Perry Mason, Cagney and Lacey, and the entire universe gets on the job. Even Amber of Amber Alert fame was a white girl, because, as it seems, white women must be found at all costs, which unfortunately inadvertently says that white women's lives are more valuable.

Because she was white and young, and found in an unsavory part of town, it was assumed our Annie was a prostitute. But if she were a man, would he be considered a pimp? If she were a different color player in the game, would so much effort be made to discover her identity?

But for a lost woman of color, far too often the families are left to collect clues on their own. If you're not Mrs. White, getting police and media assistance seems to require sheer luck . . . more like the roll of the dice.

We cannot make assumptions about people because we just don't know. We must collect all the facts of the case. Usually, we never really have enough information to make a judgment about someone else's life anyway: who they really are, and why they do the things they do. We can't judge a (math) book by its cover.

Just as the unsavory accusations about Annie were ultimately urban legends, there are a myriad of reasons why she could have been in a position to be found in that river, or to be taking the sketchy city bus, so to speak.

When we assume, we've basically made notes and collected information on our proverbial detective pad. We zero in on a conclusion, and we present our findings and judgments. In the game, we formulate an accusation, and then we open the *Clue* envelope to reveal the truth, to solve the mystery.

But it's often more complicated than that. In Annie's case, we will never know, and that's just how it is sometimes . . . we don't always get closure or answers. In my case, evidence was mounting that I was different, but I often misjudged my own behavior and beat myself up for things I later found I had no control over.

Turns out—being "inattentive" is often a clue of ADHD, which presented for me as the lack of attention in school due to boredom (hello, "We Don't Give a Shit" group?). The inability to read a room, unfiltered comments, embarrassing but sometimes preventable predicaments were all part of it.

But just like Loverboy mentions in the "Working for the Weekend" lyrics, *"Everybody needs a second chance."* If we're lucky, that's exactly what we get . . . a second chance. Annie was lucky enough to get one—and all those who are CPR certified definitely *give a shit* about that second chance.

chapter six

Investigation & Scrutinization

Careful examination of the information to solidify facts

I ran into my grandparents' dining room, shaking my napkin frantically and yelling, "DO NOT eat the salad!"

My grandfather, whom I called "Pap," was in the middle of telling a story about getting caught in a sand trap during his latest golf game, and he dropped his fork. He stared at me, immediately assessing my panic.

At the time, he was between chemotherapy sessions and apparently feeling unnaturally spry. He leapt from the table like Eric Liddell in *Chariots of Fire*, throwing his plate into the trash can with gusto and precision as if it were a discus in the Olympics. He fled for the kitchen and upon his return brought a new package of fine china wannabe dinnerware. Read: paper plates, which he proudly presented as if it were a newborn baby.

For the removal of the offending salad, he grabbed some completely unnecessary potholders for the chilled salad bowl and treated the procedure like he was removing the water on the knee bucket piece from Hasbro's *Operation* game. Concentrating with a furrowed brow, he gingerly swooped it up as if removing a rodent from a punchbowl with a pair of kitchen tongs. I realize now that Pap clearly passed down his flair for the dramatic, but Grandma, on the other hand, didn't move. She still had her original plate, containing a mountain of salad.

My grandparents had moved to San Diego from Marin County upon retirement, onto another golf course. On this particular trip, I was visiting them alone. My grandma, who was pretty much *over* cooking dinner, like, as in, *for good*, was happy for me to try out my cooking "skills" (subjective) in her kitchen.

Pap was ill with lymphoma at the time, and I didn't want to accidentally poison him, so I negotiated ordering pizza, offering to make a salad and garlic bread. My grandparents thought this was a fine compromise and didn't even mind when I suggested disposable plates and utensils. All the better aerodynamically for my grandfather's plate moonlighting as a discus, incidentally.

I had taken "foods" class in junior high school and had begun occasionally (and by occasionally, I mean, like maybe three other times) helping with dinner. The offending dish was a salad I had made in the past that had received positive reviews all three times I made it. I couldn't Google the recipe, but I felt sure I could remember the correct ingredients and measurements for the dressing.

To this day I'm not exactly sure what happened, but using my keen investigative skills, I can only assume I accidentally put in two teaspoons of garlic *salt* instead of garlic *powder*. So we all sat down to eat dinner, gathered around the open pizza boxes with our paper plates, and I brought out the "no-fail" (yet) salad. Amid conversation, we scooped heaping mountains of dressing-drenched lettuce pieces onto our plates and passed the salad bowl around the table. The prayer had been said, the plastic cutlery was poised, and we began to eat.

INVESTIGATION & SCRUTINIZATION

I took one bite of the salad and nearly choked. Immediately my face flushed, and I grabbed for my water, which I began chugging with full force. I threw my napkin violently over my face and began coughing into it, eventually standing up to leave the room so that my grandparents didn't have to listen to me hacking away.

After my grandpa and I had tossed our plates and the offensive-enough-to-warrant-theatrics salad bowl had been removed, I settled back into my seat.

"I already had some salad!" my grandmother exclaimed gleefully. She continued, "There's absolutely nothing wrong with it. I thought it was quite good, in fact!" She wouldn't look me in the eye, but she sounded confident.

Okay, what? There was actually no possible way on God's green earth that she was serious.

I cocked my head to the side and said firmly, "No, Grandma. Just, no—you don't have to be polite. That was disgusting, and I'd be horrified if you kept on eating it."

I watched her take another bite of salad, holding myself back from smacking the fork right out of her hand to save her. I watched her face flush, and she raised her napkin to her lips while she let out a gentle stifled series of little coughs and took a sip of water.

"See? I knew it was terrible! Feel free to spit it out—just go spit it out!" I commanded and valiantly pointed to the bathroom.

Grandma shook her head and looked at me. "No, it's absolutely just fine! Please, sit down!" Her voice cracked as she spoke, but she didn't waver.

Uhm. What the—? I decided to try one last time.

"Grandma. Let me level with you. I can't stand to sit here and watch you eat that salty salad. I know you're just being nice; it's totally not necessary, although I appreciate you trying to spare my feelings. It's disgusting, it's gross, and you're going to be so bloated tomorrow you won't be able to show up at church because you won't be able to fit into any of your clothes. Please. May I please take your plate away and get you a new one?" I tried to ensure my tone was kind and less demanding.

She shook her head, and I watched in absolute horror as she took another bite of the salad, repeating the same process: her face flushed, napkin to the lips, stifled series of gentle little old lady coughs.

I shook my head. I wondered why she was doing this to me when I was trying to save her. I didn't realize my grandma was still carrying some habits from her Depression-era childhood. Namely, nothing ever went to waste. I wasn't sure which was more awkward, the fact that she completely denied the existence of the Saltapalooza Salad from Hell or the fact that I was basically begging this woman not to eat it.

Guess who was a no-show at church the next day?

But don't worry, my grandma managed to rally for the local rodeo (yes, a San Diegan rodeo, shrug), and I always admired their effort to plan fun activities. For instance, I recalled a previous visit when they shuttled my younger brother, Scott, and me to a water park. After changing into our swimsuits, we stuffed our clothes into a shared locker that unbeknownst to us was inhabited by ants.

We discovered this unfortunate fact when we went to change before leaving, and it gave all new meaning to the phrase "ants in your pants." Pap's solution was to wrap us in towels and hang our pants out of the hatchback of the Chevy Cavalier station wagon. Incidentally, that car was destined to be mine when I turned sixteen. So there we were, two kids and two senior citizens bombing down the freeway, blasting the Glenn Miller Orchestra on cassette, with two pairs of pants flying behind the car like windsocks. By the time we pulled into the garage, the *slacks*, as my grandmother called them, were undoubtedly insect-free.

Those poor ants didn't stand a chance.

I'll never forget how on one visit, we decided to zip into the movies before my flight home. I remember standing outside the theater, pondering which movie to see. We read the marquee and the descriptions from a newspaper tucked under my grandfather's arm, finally settling on *Aladdin*, as the other choices were *White Men Can't Jump* and *Single White Female*, both of which seemed a bit out of our comfort zone. I had zero desire to spend two hours whisper-explaining race and basketball culture or accidentally watching a sex scene with my grandparents, thank you very much. *Aladdin* proved to be the genie in a bottle.

My grandma made a beeline for the concession stand, as she had this interesting habit of wanting to eat her popcorn before the movie started. Before entering the dark theater, where my nose would surely be subjected to smelling popcorn—which wasn't all that bad, of course—I distinctly remembered inhaling the lovely smell of the fresh coastal air. It was such a nice change from our new movie theater back home in Mountain View.

We had a brand-new movie theater, located next to a shiny new concert venue called Shoreline Amphitheater. This entire entertainment complex was built on top of a landfill, causing intermittent whiffs of poop. We'd be sitting in a movie and suddenly get a whiff of what smelled like raw sewage. When you were outside, depending on the wind, you might feel as if your nostrils were duct-taped to the exhaust vent of a porta potty, the smell was so intense.

This seems like the right time for a reminder of what we used to go through to see movies. I didn't have my driver's license yet, so I was still in that stage of almost but still not quite independent, which is undeniably annoying for all. So planning a movie night and arranging transportation to and from the theater became quite the project.

In some cases, the showtimes for the movie we wanted to see were listed in the newspaper. But, if the flick was a new arrival, we had to *call* the theater for showtimes. After spending approximately seventeen minutes on hold listening to *Sailing* by Christopher Cross, a prerecorded message would finally start. It was an hour-by-hour breakdown of every single movie title and time at the theater that day. Bear in mind, if the times didn't work for you (or for your parents who may be driving), you would have to call several different theaters and write down all the times and locations.

Heaven help you if you got mixed up and wrote down the theater or the time wrong. If your mom dropped you off at the AMC but you realized that the movie you wanted to see was at Century Theatres, you faced parental wrath like no other. At a minimum, a lecture for sure. About wasting their time—Did we think they had nothing better to do than to just drive us around town? The bigger risk was the possibility of the angry parent calling the whole thing off; after all, it was probably time for *60 Minutes*.

When the movie ended, another phase of the process began. We'd line up outside the phone booth to make collect calls home. A collect call was usually necessary because we had no money left for the pay phone after tickets and popcorn.

When the operator connected the call, there was that silent moment provided for callers to state their name. We'd just yell, "MOVIE'S OVER!" into the phone then hang up. That way, no one ever paid, and the parents knew to come pick us up. Pretty baller detective work, if you ask me.

I cannot imagine the inconvenience and suffering we went through before cell phones. Save for the death of the prank phone call, reliving those days is truly a nightmare. The pain of not having something we never knew we needed (and didn't exist yet) is felt more now than ever now that we have one. I remember the pain of waiting in line outside the Shoreline movie theater, breathing in the scent of fecal matter. I remember the pain of being stuck in several teenage debacles where I desperately could have used a cell phone. Beginning when I took driver's education class.

Back then, in California, at my high school at least, classroom driver's ed class was not offered. Therefore, teens (with thirty-eight key chains) who were eager to drive had to take private driver's ed classes offered through various "legitimate" channels (subjective). My class was somehow a subsidiary of Sears; I imagine today's equivalent would be like if Amazon offered driver's ed. (I'm not saying Sears was the Amazon of back then, okay? I'm just trying to point out the concept. A third party.)

I remember showing up to driver's ed class at a shed (literally a shed with electricity, people) in the bowels of San Jose. The class was divided into a few all-day Saturday sessions. Our instructor was a fiftyish, beer-bellied individual with Coke-bottle glasses, long sideburns, and slicked-back gray hair, named Max. The first couple Saturdays went fine; we sat in creaky old metal folding chairs and watched *Red Asphalt* on VHS for hours after taking Scantron quizzes that mimicked the California DMV's licensing test. Max would drone on with mildly entertaining stories featuring his own driving habits in his 1988 Hyundai Sonata. No biggie.

On the third Saturday, my mom wasn't available to drive me to the class, so my dad was given the responsibility for the morning. We ambled down the 280 freeway south from middle-class Mountain View (it was back then) toward downtown San Jose in silence. Eventually, we reached the shed. Thanking my dad for the ride, I slid off the vinyl seat and out of the vehicle, slammed the ridiculously heavy door of the gray Limited-Edition Buick LeSabre, and walked up to the ramshackle entrance.

I tried the fire-engine red doorknob. Flecks of scarlet paint floated into the air as I jiggled it left and right. Now, I'm not the sharpest crayon in the box, so it did take me a good minute to work out that the door was, in fact, locked. It was then I saw the note. Taped to the frame of the door was a torn piece of binder paper, ripped from a spiral notebook. Scrawled in Sharpie, in Max's all-caps, shaky writing, I read:

> DRIVER'S CLASS HAS MOVED.
> SORRY.
> —MAX B.

An address was listed under his signature. I spun around, only to witness the family car pause at a stoplight for five seconds. As I watched, the light turned green, and I saw the taillights of the LeSabre (which Scott and I later named "Hi, Ho, Silver") screeching around the corner.

Like a fool, I still ran after him, arms waving, yelling "Stop!" Um, yeah. Well, that was, as you can imagine, unsuccessful. I don't blame him. I'd want to get out of this particular part of San Jose as quickly as possible too.

Panic rose as I wracked my brain trying to figure out what to do next. Remember, these were the days before cell phones, and I had only about five dollars in my pocket. No change for the pay phone, nobody home to take my call. I waited for a while to see if any other students in the class showed up. Apparently, I was the last one to arrive that morning. It was also possible Max had mentioned the class moving during the last session, and I had been spacing out. Both were strong probabilities.

Eventually, I accepted the fact that no one else was coming and I was on my own. I didn't know whether to cry or just get moving. I heaved a sigh, grabbing the paper off the door frame. It was my only clue. I realized my only hope for cracking this case was to take to the streets. About a block away, I found a gas station. In the pre-GPS days, gas station attendants basically accepted that part of their job description was to give directions to lost souls in need of guidance.

Unfortunately for me, the gas station attendant did not speak English, and my high school Spanish wasn't sufficient for a conversation of this magnitude. That lead turned out to be a dead end. I continued down the street and found a Burger King, where I waved Max's note in the manager's face and asked if he could help me. He had an ancient, grease-stained navigational tool called a *Thomas Guide* (an encyclopedia of maps) behind the counter. It was the break I needed. We looked up the new location for the class. As shady and scary as this sounds, it was a motel a few blocks away. Taking pity on me, the manager scribbled down some directions, gave me a free soda, and sent me on my way.

What was probably a twenty-minute walk felt like hours. I felt like a rookie beat cop as I made my way past abandoned shopping carts, dodged random piles of garbage on the street, and stepped over old copies of the *San Jose Mercury News*. I could almost hear David Addison from *Moonlighting* in my head playing "The Long and Winding Road" on the harmonica.

Finally, I saw the illuminated neon sign for the "E-Z 8 Motel." This could NOT be right. I stood there, glancing down at the note and back up at the street number several times. It was one of those drive-up motels, and in the middle was a patch of fake green grass turf, the kind you put outside your motorhome when you roll into the RV park. Maybe . . . maybe that's what the place was.

I shuddered, already feeling like I needed a shower, but I walked up the cement stairs toward an area that loosely resembled a conference room. Slowly, I opened the door a few inches. I heard the familiar tinny sound of a police siren blaring on TV, which was strangely comforting. *Red Asphalt* was playing. The door was in desperate need of some WD-40, so a loud creak announced my presence. I pushed it all the way open, and there was Max in all his Coke-bottle, slicked-back hair, beer-bellied glory, next to a TV-VCR combo.

I knew the case was closed when I saw Max with a big smile spread across his face. He paused *Red Asphalt*. Smokey Robinson and the Miracles' "Ooo Baby Baby" was playing softly in the background over the speakers in the would-be conference room.

We discovered later that the volume could not be turned any lower, and the manager of the motel had no idea how to turn the radio off. So, it didn't matter what we were doing, watching a movie, listening to Max, taking a test—the radio was always on. What a complete shitshow.

"Well, looks like you found us, little lady! I was starting to get worried!" Max bellowed.

I wanted to shout, *"Seriously? You friggin' idiot! What the hell happened to having class in the shed? You seriously just let a fifteen-year-old girl walk, alone, through one of the nastiest parts of San Jose? And what the eff are we all doing in this godforsaken hourly rate hotel?"*

Instead, I just gave a weak smile, sat down, and wiped my sweaty brow with the edge of my "UCLA Alumni" sweatshirt. "Well," I said, "I barely made it. Are you going to change locations on us again?"

Max shook his head. "Oh, uh, no . . ." He awkwardly shuffled some papers around on his podium and then said without looking up, "I'm really sorry about that. There was a, um, eh, er, a plumbing problem at the last place, but uh . . . thankfully, my friend had this great conference room we could meet in, so I think we'll just stay here." Case closed.

Mm-hmm, super.

As a parent of multiple young adults who have smartphones and have taken driver's ed, I wonder what it would have been like for them to be in my shoes. No way to call someone and ask for help. No way to ensure their safety. The liability and the lawsuits that would certainly follow if driver's ed classes today were led to a second location without parental knowledge.

Reflecting on my teenage years now, I must hand it to my parents. What a great job they did during such an unknown time. My mom always set me up to be prepared for anything, as evidenced by my bottomless Mary Poppins carpet bag purse. My dad, on the other hand, took care of my car needs. Every time my car had an issue, my dad would roll on down to the Pick-n-Pull or Kragen Auto Parts to scavenge for car parts. Our garage was filled with random alternators, radiators, mufflers, transmissions, and God only knows what else. But you know what? To this day, I have never even had to change a flat tire.

Prior to the '90s, parents had no phone tracking, no apps to relay the location or the speed your kid was driving. In my teen years, there was jumping into cars with people I'd never met, and we'd be off to destinations unknown. There were weekends away at church camps, friend's *uncle's* cabins, and other scary-sounding places belonging to strangers or potential ne'er-do-wells. No way to contact someone in case of an emergency. I imagine they had so many sleepless nights, so many helpless thoughts, so many instances of having to give up the illusion of control. They were forced to stand constantly at the intersection of Letting Go Lane and Cling Harder Avenue.

I wonder what went through Annie's parents' minds when she never came home for dinner. Were they desperately and actively looking for her? Did they have a warm bed waiting for her, yet in the morning, it was still untouched?

Let's scrutinize the rites of passage they would have done with her in Paris during that time. Not driver's ed but maybe walk her down the aisle and see her have babies? Building memories, teaching her how to cook, or how to make a salty salad. Taking her to her grandparents' house for a visit. None of that was to be any longer, and none of it would take place in the future.

I wonder if Annie felt understood. Felt supported and loved? I'm sure she wanted what we all want—acceptance from her parents and unconditional love. To feel safe and protected. Cracking the case of the missing driver's ed class was petrifying, but I knew I had a safe home waiting for me. I knew people would miss me if I disappeared.

Who missed Annie?

chapter seven

Calling for Backup

Enlisting the assistance of others

"Uh-uh—puh-uh-uh-eeenis!" erupted Pablo, sitting next to me in Spanish class senior year. It sounded a little like a sneeze this time, but not quite.

Pablo (which was not his real name, but like the *Clue* characters, we each had a pseudonym that we were made to select in Spanish class) was a champion of the penis game during class. He could expertly cough or sneeze and loudly slide in the word "penis" in the most nonchalant, unassuming manner. Much to the delight of myself and the squad of mischief makers in the back row.

Pablo and I became fast friends when we found each other laughing and snickering at the same things. He was such a perfect penis game player that Senora Valdez would stop teaching, turn around, only to face students with straight faces and pencils poised. She'd wait for a second or two and then decide she heard it wrong or that no one actually said anything. She'd turn back to the board and continue making a chart on how to conjugate *el preterito*.

Senora Valdez wore the most eclectic outfits I'd ever seen. Usually, a pair of jeans and a T-shirt, then a white-winged dove Stevie Nicks–type caftan, and always a beret paired with a scarf tied around her neck. Of course, my classmates and I said she looked like Mr. Furley from *Three's Company*.

Pablo was the best part of the class. We found the dumbest things hilarious. Like the way our entire class refused to attempt to say anything with a Spanish accent. Instead, what came out was an entire classroom of teens saying, *"Tu tienes una computadora"* with a Valley Girl accent . . . or Valley *Teen* accent, if you will. As in from San Fernando Valley and not from Mexico or Spain.

Pablo was my partner in crime in the contribution of original artwork in the Spanish book, *Vamonos! Libro de Espanol*. This was back in the day when kids received a copy of their textbook for the class on the first day of school, so in most cases, the textbooks were used. Pablo and I made fun of all the cheesy photographs and decided to, ahem, *improve* upon the photos by adding some *customized* captions and speech bubbles.

For example, for a picture of an old man lovingly peering down at his dog, we'd draw a speech bubble by the guy that said, "Please stop licking your own balls. Sharing is caring. It's my turn."

For a picture of a man giving a speech at a podium, we'd draw a speech bubble that said, "Thank you for attending the Bedwetters Anonymous Meeting. Don't forget to grab your gift bag on the way out; it contains our newest rubber sheet."

We thought we were an unstoppable comedy team. And we were. Until the end of the year when we went to turn in our Spanish books. We were supposed to stack them nicely on the table in front of Senora Valdez so her TA could mark them off as *collected* while we took our final.

Pablo and I looked at each other, and for a moment, I panicked, thinking I was going to get in trouble.

Pablo merely shook his head and said, "No way, Jose," and reached for my textbook.

Casually, he stacked the two books on Senora Valdez's desk with the others. We assumed we were in the clear. Unfortunately for us, the TA was meticulous and spotted our shenanigans immediately. Both Pablo and I were pulled aside right after the final and given "the twenty-four-hour lecture" by Senora Valdez. She popped our textbooks and a bottle of Wite-Out in each of our hands and instructed us to go home and eradicate the speech bubbles by the next day or she would call our parents.

Needless to say, that was a fool's errand. I was out of Wite-Out by page fourteen. In the end, we both paid for our books and agreed it was unfortunate that Senora Valdez didn't have a sense of humor.

Her loss.

Aside from Pablo, choir was one of the bright spots in high school. My high school life was a bit of a Shakespearean tragedy (if only in my own mind) in that I really didn't feel like I had close friends at school. My good friends were in my church youth group, but what I really wanted was a place of belonging at school. It's where I spent most of my days. But most of the time, it seemed no one was accepting applications for new members to their friend groups.

I've been searching for connections my whole life, basically. From my spin around the multilevel marketing world when I sold Lankersheim baskets (while everyone else was selling PartyLite candles and Joelle Cosmetics) to family reunions on cruise ships with matching T-shirts where everyone was out doing the macarena on the lido deck, to the time I wanted to try Renaissance-themed live action role playing.

It's the same concept of the people who collect postcards and form clubs, purchase mascot gear and gather for the furry conventions, or put the white rocks in front of their polyamorous swinger-friendly houses.

I mean, *"Sometimes you wanna go where everybody knows your name . . . and they're always glad you came."*

Everyone needs a place to belong, a place to feel valued on this ball of mud hurling through the stratosphere. I found mine with the choir heads, in the shadow of the altos, sopranos, tenors, and bases. Choir allowed me to experience that feeling of connection, closeness, and bonding. Where your heart swells and you feel that warm, fuzzy, blissful rush. Your burdens are lighter, you're sharing inside jokes, you are giddy, accepted, willing to help anybody with anything involving the group. Doing things out of a desire to be of service and not out of obligation, knowing that being of service is going to build those connections tighter and more of them. For me, connectedness was, and still is, a drug.

Choir provided that sense of belonging. Just like church, choir was a massively important entity and community for me for many years. It was that sense of being seen, being known, being necessary, being missed if you didn't show up.

One day in choir, it was announced to us that our sister high school in Japan was offering to host us on an overseas adventure, singing and performing for their school students and city officials. We'd pay for the flights, but when we arrived on Japanese soil, they'd match each of us up with a host student and stay in their family's home.

To earn the necessary funds for the trip, our school choir did some fairly wild things, at least by today's standards. We were encouraged to go door to door, hitting up people for cash donations. We were also provided with long lists of phone numbers and instructed to make cold calls to district parents, asking for money. In all honesty, those occasionally turned into *prank* calls. We *may have* asked a few people if they'd like to purchase glow-in-the-dark condoms that said "Mountain View HS" when extended to full length.

We even pimped ourselves out to local convalescent homes to do holiday concerts. We would pass the hat to collect donations at the end of our performances. Those visits are still alive in my memory. As soon as we walked into the facility, the stench of urine and disinfectant filled the air. Somebody would always start coughing and overreacting to the smell. We may have sounded like angels when we sang, but we were really just a bunch of smart-ass kids.

Our standard-issue choir uniform was a shimmery white button-down shirt, black dress slacks (I hate that word) for the boys and full-length black skirts for the girls. We had gold metallic cummerbunds and bowties. We looked either like knockoff Gladys Knight & the Pips or like we were about to audition for *The Starlight Express*, your choice.

Our choir director, Martha Shuce, would blow into her pitch pipe to give us our starting note. We were always scrambling and shuffling in a sloppy lineup until we heard that first note. We'd try to curtail our conversations and stifle our snickers as we sang "Jingle Bells," "Silent Night," and other favorites. I can honestly say if you haven't spent at least one afternoon clowning around in an old folk's home, singing "Hava Nagila" with your peers, it should be on the bucket list.

During one particularly memorable visit at a convalescent home, our singing was interrupted by an indignant orderly exclaiming, "Oh! Now, Mr. Graham, you can't do that in here. You know better!" as she hurriedly removed a gentleman in a wheelchair whose hands were moving fiercely under the blanket in his lap. Apparently inspired by our glittery, youthful goodies, Mr. Graham was treating himself to some afternoon delight, right in the middle of our performance.

Despite ourselves and Mr. Graham, we raised the cash for our trip to Japan. A bunch of bratty, irreverent rich kids from Silicon Valley headed across the globe to represent our school. We were required to have a week of "cultural training" before the administration would allow us to have a plane ticket. In retrospect, this was both understandable and wise.

The success of the cultural training is anyone's guess—pretty subjective.

Forty students and seven adults from Mountain View boarded a United Airlines flight and settled in for fourteen fun-filled hours of hair braiding, travel *Clue* game investigating, Weird Al song accordion playing, movie watching, yo-yo "dog walking," Mad Libs writing, airplane food throwing, gum chewing, Rubik's Cube twisting, chubby bunny gaming hours.

This was long before the "mile high club" was a thing for us, so no one monitored how many people crowded into the airplane lavatory. A derivative of "Seven Minutes in Heaven" was concocted somewhere in international airspace, and the urban legend was that possibly some babies were conceived. Interestingly, that "strange rash" so many students contracted a month after the trip turned out to be an outbreak of mononucleosis. What a coincidence.

As you can probably guess, no one slept a *wink* the entire flight. Not us teenagers, who were having the unsupervised time of our lives. Not the other passengers, who were openly and obviously annoyed. And certainly not the chaperones, who were adjusting their earplugs, pretending to be asleep under eye masks. Secretly, they were probably taking generous pulls off coffee cups full of free booze and rethinking their decisions to attend this ten-day international field trip.

Boarding the bus after deplaning and collecting our bags at customs, we congratulated ourselves for getting this far. We continued our irritating antics as we ooo'd and aah'd at the burgundy velvet curtains and plush leather bus seats, and we burst into giggles when we noticed the bus had crystal *Phantom of the Opera* chandeliers hanging from the ceiling.

"This is like this porno I saw once!" said Les King. "There was an orgy, and there were like four naked Japanese girls per white guy, and they were all taking turns—"

"LES!" fumed a jet-lagged Mrs. Shuce. "THIS is not the time or place! Now sit down and shut up!" she hissed.

Through the night, we drove until we reached the high school and were greeted by hundreds of screaming kids. Our bus pulled up and they lost their minds. Literally jumping on any protruding pieces of the bus, mirrors, windshield wipers, steps, and taillights. It was as if Michael Jackson's tour bus had arrived. Any relaxing and sleepyheaded drooping eyes were instantly invigorated and revived as the energy of the welcome pierced the night sky.

Mrs. Shuce, who looked like she had aged about forty-six years in the past two days, read off the host family assignments, and we exited the bus, one at a time, each student receiving roaring cheers as the bus door opened and the hydraulic lift released, and the stair lowered. *PSSHHH.*

I was placed with Noriko Kobayashi's family, and they were about the kindest, most gracious people you could ever meet. They embraced me as if Noriko and I were twins separated at birth. I was surprised by the excitement and visual displays of affection, as I had been under the impression the Japanese weren't the type to react in an overexuberant manner. They drove us home, fed us some fascinating foods, but we were all starving, and it didn't matter much what it was... and then they let us bathe and sleep.

In theory, we were supposed to shadow our host student and do exactly what they did: if they rode a bike to school, we rode one with them. When they went to class, we went to class. We ate what they ate, we did what they did, but as time went on, it became clear that some minor adjustments needed to be made.

The next day, our first activity at the sister high school in Japan was to attend a banquet in our honor. We were served an interesting dinner—a bento box that contained what looked to be raw ground beef, some vegetables, and rice. After choking down a little bit of food, we were scheduled to go onstage and sing a number we had learned in Japanese called "Sakura." In return, the Japanese student band was going to play a Metallica song for us. Okay. Good. Sounds great.

Did I mention I was the choir president that year? (Read: choir chump assigned to meaningless tasks that were supposed to represent "leadership" for no reward or recognition.) Therefore, it was my job to get onstage and introduce our choir and our choir director and say a little something about our song. Like how apparently *sakura* means "cherry blossoms."

At our scheduled time, we climbed up onto the stage and haphazardly shuffled into our formation. Still jet-lagged and ridiculously tired, we were all a few ingredients short of a sushi roll that night. Choir Director Martha Shuce handed me the microphone, smiled, and nodded firmly to me in a way that subliminally said, *Don't screw this up, Carlton.*

I took the mic and a deep breath and turned to face the room filled with Japanese students, administrators, and school officials. The chatter had died down, and the only noise in the room was the sound of chopsticks clicking on the bento boxes.

"Hi," I began. At that moment, through the fog of excitement and jet lag, I realized I didn't have a plan. I needed a plan for this! I should have practiced. Not realizing that no one spoke fluent English, I just launched into a nervous impromptu speech, which I delivered at warp speed.

"I'mAmyFromMountainViewHighSchoolThanksForHavingUsTonightThisIsTheMountainViewHighSchoolChoirOurNameIsTouchOfClassHeyIHearYouGuysAreGonnaPlayEnterSandmanByMetallicaForUs?CoolOhAndThisIsOurDirectorShuceSensei."

I spun around, looking for the microphone stand. In my panic, I accidentally pointed the mic directly toward the speaker. Remember the movie *Splash*? There was a scene where Madison was in Bloomingdales watching the wall of TVs. She said her name, which was a high-pitched squeal that sounded like *Flipper* the dolphin. The sound shattered the glass of every tube in the store.

Similarly, the conclusion of my incoherent, two-second speech was an earsplitting blast of feedback. This was followed by audible shrieks from the audience and my fellow choir members alike. I physically cringed on stage, with my back still to the audience. Slowly, I turned to face them, hoping to gauge the reaction from my public speaking efforts. In my humble opinion, I had nailed it.

Every person in the entire room was covering their ears with both hands. Some jaws had dropped. Some were wincing; others were scowling. All were silent, no applause. I suddenly realized that no one in this room of non-English speakers caught one single word of my speech. My face flushed and my palms started sweating. I tried to slyly wipe them on my palazzo pants, but they were about as absorbent as a soaking wet sponge.

Just then, the Japanese school Principal Takahashi came onstage, smiling from ear to ear. He grabbed the mic, turned to us, and bowed several times. Yes! I knew about bowing. I started bowing, too, as we were instructed to do at our training. Then I took note of his outfit: he was dressed to kill in a white tuxedo with matching top hat, as if he was trying to be Phil Collins in the "Don't Lose My Number" video. He looked sharp.

Principal Takahashi spoke very slowly and clearly in English, and everyone in the audience was smiling and nodding, catching every word. Well, dang; that's how it's done. He finished his speech by announcing the band and pulling the curtain back as "Enter Sandman" began blasting from the guitar amp, accompanied by the bass and the drums.

I guess my emcee skills needed a little practice.

The next day, I realized why Principal Takahashi wore the white tux: the school color was white. Naturally, that meant the uniforms were white. What an impractical color for a school uniform—Am I white?

On that trip to Japan, I decided biking was no longer for me. Biking to school through the streets of Iwata is still one of the scariest experiences I've had to date. Horns honking, people yelling in Japanese, cars everywhere in no particular lane. And shhh, don't tell my mom, but there were *no bike helmets*. She's gonna kill me when she reads this.

By the time we made it to the school each day, I felt like the inspiration for the term "rode hard and put away wet." Pitting out under my arms, mud splatter on my skirt, and windblown Bea Arthur hair. More evidence that I was not a down girl.

As American students, we weren't used to the length of the Japanese school day, so many interesting things took place. There were *no janitors*, for example. The faculty called upon the students to clean the campus! If that weren't shocking enough, math class was fascinating.

The teacher started out by briefly explaining a concept and pointing to a math problem on the chalkboard that had been left there by a student in the previous class. After the explanation, the students bowed their heads and pencils, connecting mind and hand to paper. After a moment, a student's hand shot up in the back row. The sensei made his way over to her and inspected her paper. He gave her a pleasant-sounding response; she rose and went to the front of the class.

Another student's hand shot up as he finished. The first student made her way over to his desk and pointed, making a few comments; he erased something and wrote something, and the female student nodded. Then the male stood up and moved to attend to the next boy who had his hand up to call for backup.

They say you retain much more when you teach something, as opposed to simply audibly learning something and regurgitating it. How true I have found that to be in my own experience. It was fascinating to watch this class function separately but also together as a unit.

After regular Japanese school was out, they wanted us to participate in an additional four hours of learning and activity each afternoon. Foreign language, concentrations in two additional phonetic scripts, cramming for entrance exams, physical exercise, and practicing of forty-six characters.

Our chaperones quickly realized it was going to be, as Wadsworth says in the *Clue* movie, a *red herring*. We had not been conditioned for this type of torture! We couldn't keep ourselves quiet and still for all that time. By day three, after finding a group (not including me, by the way) sneaking off campus to purchase cigarettes across the street, the chaperones gave up. What can I say? Our rebellion game was strong.

For the rest of the trip, we could be found outside, practicing the macarena, playing *The Legend of Zelda* on someone's Nintendo Game & Watch, or playing those old-school kid clapping and rhyming games like Miss Susie and Miss Mary Mack. We grabbed chalk and left our mark all over the Japanese asphalt with our endless games of M*A*S*H* (Mansion, Apartment, Shack, House—come on, I know you played it too).

When we managed to completely escape the watchful eyes of adults, we crowded under the cherry blossom tree, congregating around a single yellow Sony Walkman, listening to the new LL Cool J and Boyz II Men song "Hey Lover" and trying to decipher all the inappropriate lyrics.

It was behind that tree that a classmate (who shall remain nameless) shoved their tongue down my throat, then ran it across my retainer, which was a disgustingly awkward attempt at the romantic move of the century. The person attempting to make out with me had orthodontia, too, and there was food stuck in his braces. It tasted like he had been to Sizzler just moments ago, and the evidence was still stuck in his Rainbow Brite brackets because lunch was lodged around the braces and in the wires. These were the days prior to the ability to get colored wire on your braces, honey, so you *knew* it was food. It was, hands down, *the* worst kiss ever.

When the interminable school day was finally over and our host students could finally leave, we erupted like the *Space Invaders* Atari game, just taking off running helter-skelter for the bikes. Or maybe more like MC Hammer in the "U Can't Touch This" video because of the white outfits, moving like a family of the least graceful doves you'd ever seen. Doves on bikes. In Japan. Who looked like MC Hammer. I *know* you know what I mean.

Just like in the Japanese math class, Annie became a teacher, unconventional as she may have seemed to be. First, Dr. James Elam discovered that he could keep the blood temporarily oxygenated, and perfected that technique, eventually calling it cardiopulmonary resuscitation. But he was going to need a prototype, an educational aid.

As they say, it was teamwork that made the dream work. And eventually, Annie taught others to give life . . . through her death. Stay tuned.

chapter eight

Probable Cause & Reasonable Suspicion

Collecting clues and identifying suspects
for the purpose of building a case

The Azusa Pacific University choir was touring through the Bay Area and stopped at my church when I was in elementary school. The choir girls had this big, gorgeous hair, and they looked like they had their shit together, standing up there onstage in their makeup and their matching Golden Girls' dresses. I remember thinking, *Someday, I'm going to go to college there.*

And I did.

We had arranged for my family to move me into the dorms early, as we were planning on dropping off my stuff and heading off on a vacation. In order to get my dorm key early, I had to drop into the Campus Safety office, since registration wasn't officially open yet.

I walked in only to find a few officers crowded around a beautiful Black lady sitting at a desk. A small TV set, with antennas pointing north and west, was perched on the counter, and I could hear "Bad Boys" by Inner Circle coming through the speaker. You didn't need to see the screen to know it was clearly an episode of *Cops*.

"Now, you see that? That's illegal now; you can't escalate to that hold unless you can prove that level of use of force is necessary in a court of law," the woman instructed as she pointed to the screen. She looked amazing in her black-and-gray uniform, badge, and Sally Browne belt—polished . . . almost regal.

I stood there awkwardly for a moment, just staring at her.

Feeling the weight of my stare, she looked up at me with piercing dark brown eyes. "May I help you?" she asked.

I cleared my throat. "Uh, yes. I'm here to get the key for Engstrom 402?"

"Last name?" she asked.

"Carlton," I replied. I stared at her name tag. Brooks. Linda Brooks.

Officer Linda Brooks picked up a clipboard and flipped through it, grabbed a highlighter, and without looking up, took the cap off. As neon yellow met paper, Linda Brooks said, "I'll need to see some ID, Miss Carlton."

I fumbled around in my purse, searching through forty-three pens, receipts, pieces of scratch paper, lipsticks, and hair ties, finally producing a driver's license. I handed it to her, and before I even could process the words coming out of my mouth, I blurted out, "Are you guys hiring right now?"

Officer Brooks looked up at me and pointed to a stack of applications in the corner of the desk on a paper tray. "Always. Take one and bring it back on Friday. That's when the chief is in. That way it won't get lost in the shuffle."

Noted.

Officer Brooks unlocked a lockbox of keys in labeled envelopes. She fished through it and handed me the envelope with my key. "Sign here," she instructed, handing me a pen and the clipboard, pointing to my last name. I signed then grabbed an application off the corner of the desk.

"Friday," repeated Officer Brooks. I nodded and thanked her, turning to leave. "Oh, and Miss Carlton?" I spun around to face her again. She smiled at me with the most beautiful white teeth I had ever seen. "Good luck," she said.

I did return the application on Friday then promptly forgot about it as the school year started up. By the time Labor Day weekend had passed, I was in full college mode: in choir camp, meeting people, going on late-night runs to "Donut Man," the donut store down the road, freshman orientation, and all the things. I had been remiss in getting my hair permed before I left for school, so it was time to get that done—after all, I was a choir girl now, and I had a reputation to uphold.

By this point, I only had eighty dollars to my name, and I knew perms were expensive. In a stroke of good fortune, I'd found a random coupon for the JCPenney hair salon on the ground by the mailboxes outside of the cafeteria. I hastily scooped it up, called, and made an appointment. Next, I had to figure out a ride, so my buddy down the hall in Engstrom 402 let me borrow her 1978 chartreuse VW Rabbit, and I was off to Montclair Plaza. I walked into the salon and asked for Jean, expecting to see a woman. It was the mid-'90s, so at that time, I mostly took things for face value.

The receptionist went back to find Jean. She came back, adjusting her ponytail and smacking her Bubblicious gum. Some old man was following her, who I figured was her grandfather, probably coming in to get his comb-over trimmed.

"Amy Carlton? I'm Gene," he said in what I dubbed an *old man voice:* a shade of raspy with a side of hoarseness.

My jaw dropped. This was not registering. Let's get real—Gene was probably all of sixty years old. But to me he looked like he had just recently climbed out of the grave at Forest Lawn and bummed a ride to work from the Ghostbusters. I mean, this geriatric hairstylist was ancient. He was probably educated by dinosaurs and went to beauty school at the La Brea Tar Pits, but I knew there was no turning back. Plus, how judgmental was I? I should give this guy a whirl. Was I really going to make a scene and be ageist?

I forced myself to relax into three hours in the chair with Gene. The Sony Watchman TV was on, and the local news reported that the prosecution was going to forgo the death penalty in favor of pursuing life without parole for the defendant if convicted . . . it was the OJ Simpson trial. Gene waved a comb at the TV set and remarked, "He's as guilty as Al Capone!"

I wasn't exactly sure what that meant, so I gave him an enthusiastic but noncommittal "Mmm!" and changed the subject, asking Gene about his homelife.

Gene rolled my hair and chatted while the perm solution dripped like a leaky faucet onto my shoulders, which were covered in a threadbare towel. He told me he grew up in Shreveport, Louisiana. He told me about his adventures during the war. He told me about his wife, Melba. He told me about his postwar occupation as an assistant helping an accountant do taxes at H&R Block. He told me about his decision five years ago to retire and the dream he had about switching gears. He decided to finish off his working years doing something creative and artistic and chose to go to beauty school to learn how to cut and color. (And hopefully, how to do perms, though he didn't mention it.)

I thought that was cool. I mean, dang, good for him! You're never too old to reinvent yourself. I mean, after all, look at Madonna, with her platinum blond short haircut after years of permed "Like a Virgin" locks. He had a really good vibe about him, and I decided I was going to give Gene the stylist the benefit of the doubt.

After hours of torture, Gene, my pounding headache, and I were all returning from the shampoo bowl when I glanced in the mirror. To my horror, I noticed immediately that my hair was lopsided. One side was significantly less curly than the other side. I didn't say a word, figuring it would look different when dry. I sat back down in the chair patiently and tried to focus on Gene's story about his recent hip replacement surgery. I practiced the Helen Keller stare in the mirror, trying to remain calm as the curled side of my hair slowly shrank as Gene chatted away over the hum of the blow-dryer and the diffuser.

Finally, the truth was clear: one side of my head was long and beach wavy, and the other side was a tight poodle perm. I looked like I was trying an asymmetrical style, like Salt-N-Pepa in the "Push It!" video. The difference was so obvious that finally Gene couldn't ignore it.

Adjusting his glasses, he ran his fingers through the curls with his hands. "Well, what in the Sam Hill?" I heard his confused tone as he pondered the problem. As if we were playing a game of *Clue* and he asked to see another player's card during the investigative phase of the game but was not expecting to see the particular card the other player revealed. With a puzzled look on his face, he continued rifling through his work and then began examining his products. Almost as if he were carefully inspecting and evaluating his plethora of detective's notes, desperately trying to get to the bottom of what happened.

Suddenly, I saw his eyebrows shoot north in the mirror, and he smiled and laughed. "Well," he said, "it looks like expired perm solution doesn't work very well after all!" He acted like he had solved the case of Professor Plum doing the effed-up perm, in the salon, with the expired chemicals.

I, on the other hand, was pissed. I mean, come on, Gene! What in the name of Colonel Mustard possessed this crazy old fool to use expired perm solution on *my* hair? Was he senile? Did he have Alzheimer's? He went on to explain how he had inherited some other stylist's old developer and neutralizer when they retired from doing hair. As if this explanation was supposed to help me to feel better about my asymmetrical perm, which had serious fourth-grade vibes from when I used to pin my hair up on one side only. But I didn't dig the one-sided look anymore. I mean shit—this was the '90s! I knew Maddie Hayes, the Blue Moon Shampoo hair model from *Moonlighting*, would never stand for this.

And neither was I . . . and *certainly* not when I was spending my *own* hard-earned money! Err, wait. Suddenly it hit me. Something my parents told me growing up repeatedly: *"You get what you pay for."*

I mentally clapped my hands in front of my face, as if I were attempting to turn off this nightmare using the "Clapper." I thought maybe it was a nightmare and I wasn't actually awake. But the smell of the perm was still burning in my nostrils. I dug deep. Maybe I could *turn on* some forced empathy for Gene before I started crying.

I considered the situation as Gene continued talking about chemicals, and it all began to fit into place. My grandmother, who was about the same age, lived through the Great Depression era. Those folks formed habits that really couldn't be unformed. She would always save Ziploc bags, wash them out, and reuse them. She lined her shelves with wrapping paper from Christmas and saved every last dinner morsel—even forcing herself to eat the Saltapalooza salad. She would put the breadsticks from a restaurant in her purse "in case she needed a snack later." Even though they lived on a golf course and were quite obviously doing fine these days.

But that kind of stuff is seared into your brain, and what can I say? Old habits die hard. I mean, that Sony Watchman playing the news about the OJ trial? In today's world, that thing would last maybe a year and be obsolete. My Pioneer car stereo cassette/CD combo in the Chevy Cavalier? That thing is probably still capable of pumping out the jams today, on display in a museum of car antiquities. Possibly in the Petersen Automotive Museum on Wilshire and Fairfax where Notorious B.I.G. killed in a drive-by.

Worthy of noting, the perm-with-Gene incident *did* solidify my decision to call Campus Safety back to ensure they had received my application, only to discover they had left three messages for me on my dorm answering machine. Whoops. I accepted the job immediately and started that very night, despite my ridiculous hair. I needed to be able to afford a better perm.

No offense to Gene.

I discovered it wasn't exactly fun and games fitting my pear-shaped hips into a man's uniform. Even the Sally Browne wasn't as comfortable as I'd expected. Once again, I found myself in the field of weight fluctuation as I battled with the "freshman fifteen" I was quickly procuring. (Over the course of my lifetime, my weight has bounced more than a book of bad checks.)

One night while watching TV, a beacon of hope appeared—a commercial for some new, legal fat-burning pills. First was Suzanne Somers' Thigh Master commercial. Followed by the commercial for *Freedom Rock*, a compilation of "four records, three cassettes, or two CDs" featuring hippies in lawn chairs sitting outside of a VW bus, having this conversation:

"Hey man, is that Freedom Rock*?"*

"Yeah, man!"

"Well, TURN IT UP, man!"

Then the overly excited (read: stoned) hippies roll out the obligatory sampler platter of assorted songs of the *Freedom Rock* era, the "forty songs by the original artists" crawling in a cheesy, generic yellow font up the screen: "Ramblin' Man" . . . "Free Bird" . . . "White Room" . . . "A Horse with No Name" . . .

And then, like the common-sense bomb of a lifetime, came the fat-burning orlistat pills commercial, like a shooting star, like manna from heaven. A pill that *prevents the body from absorbing dietary fat*?

I had to have them. I called the 800 number (yes, young folks, I had to speak to an actual human and have a conversation). They arrived without issue, but upon further investigation, I realized something as I nerded out reading the back of the bottle. The potential side effects were listed, easily visible in plain English ... one of which was "violent diarrhea." That warning didn't stop me.

A couple days into taking the pills, everything was so far, so good. I had no issues. My friend Erica was a local who lived in Glendora, the next suburb over. She asked if I wanted to go hang out with her friends from church to get some food. Well, why not?

Back in those days, crew, you did not question such things. True, I had only known Erica a couple weeks and had met her friends exactly zero times before. There were no Craigslist murders, and I had that youthful *it's-never-going-to-happen-to-me* mentality. Well, I didn't get murdered by any of those random people whom I didn't know, but what I wasn't prepared for was the possibility that my intestines could murder *me*: the crime was *homicide of intestines*. In the *bathroom*. With the *diet pill*.

Anyway, Erica picked me up shortly after my Campus Safety shift was over. I hopped into the front of her peacock-green Hyundai Elantra, saying hi to the two random guys in the back: Jack, who looked and sounded like Spicoli in *Fast Times at Ridgemont High*, and Jermaine, who reminded me of a younger version of Will Smith.

We were soon hauling buns down the 210 west. As I listened to these two guys from the Valley (not Silicon Valley, where I grew up, but the *real, actual* valley ... San Fernando) talk about *Above the Rim*, the movie with Tupac, my stomach made an audible gurgling sound, and it reverberated loudly throughout the Elantra. I could feel my face flush, grateful it was already getting dark in the car. Immediately, I involuntarily slapped myself across my stomach, as if that was going to help the situation. I bit my lip and rolled my eyes. We all laughed.

Jermaine said, "Don't worry 'bout it, girl. I'm hungry too."

I thought I might die. Hungry. *As if!*

We found street parking on Colorado and Sierra Madre. By now, I was feeling like maybe if I could just take a pin and pop my stomach, we'd be all good in the hood. But first, we were going to have to attempt to park. Pasadena parking, at least in the '90s, was well-known for its *curb conundrum*. You see, the city had these uber-tall curbs back then. The trick was you had to park just close enough to the curb where you could exit the vehicle without getting the car door wedged into the grass, or worse, the cement, God help you.

Miracle of all miracles, we parked at the perfect angle. As we bailed out, my gassy insides were feeling like a bottle about to launch a cork. I was going to have to find the restroom fast. I could feel that Mary Lou Retton herself had posted up in my guts and was performing back handsprings. Either that or my intestines were planning to audition for the Blue Man Group. Everyone else was laughing and chatting, but I was Tom Cruise on a Mission Impossible. I needed a restroom, STAT.

I scanned the surrounding establishments. Who was going to be the unfortunate victim of what I was about to do to their porcelain? I could see Moose McGillycuddy's, but it was way up there, an undetermined number of blocks away. Then, suddenly, like a lighthouse in a storm, there it was, probably only ten yards from where I stood: Lupita's. I'm pretty sure it was glowing, and I could almost hear the hallelujah chorus. I paid no mind to the busy street and started bolting across the street like Steve Martin competing with Kevin Bacon for a cab to the airport in *Planes, Trains and Automobiles*.

I scrambled to slow my roll as I reached the door. My legs looked like Scooby Doo and Shaggy's, flailing in circles from the momentum. I flung open the door with the force only seen in those desperate for a toilet. Live mariachi music filled my ears *"Ay, ay ay ay ... Canta y no llores ..."*

"¡Buenas noches, mija!" a beautiful Latina woman standing at the hostess stand smiled at me with a red-lipsticked grin that could move mountains. She gave me hope.

"Bueno!" I called while remaining in constant motion, on a quest for a door marked "Baño." I headed for the corner of the restaurant that looked the most promising. Gah! As if I were Ms. Pac-Man chasing cherries, I hit a dead end: *la cocina.*

The employees must have read the panic on my face. "Damas?" asked a young waiter as he hoisted a tray of steaming enchiladas onto his shoulder.

I swallowed hard. *"Si, por favor!"* I said breathlessly. I realized I was panting, not so much from the mad dash crossing the street but from the urgency.

"A la derecha," instructed the waiter, pointing behind me.

I spun around and saw the word "Mujeres" on the door.

What happened in that restroom was strictly between me and that toilet. It was like a one-night stand, a private bond. A moment (well about twenty-five minutes) of wanton, unbridled, loyal connectedness that was ours together, and ours alone. At least if I died on this commode, someone could just roll me out of this restaurant and into the crevice of an extra-tall Pasadena curb. That's all I can say. I won't kiss and tell. My sphincter's sealed.

When I was under control enough to leave the baño, I emerged to find Erica, Jermaine, and Jack seated at a circular table around a lazy Susan of chips and salsa. All of them stared at me with varying degrees of concern.

Jack pulled a chair up for me and patted the vinyl seat. "Good choice. I love this place! Sit down, Azusa Betty!" he said, grinning. "We've got bean dip comin'!"

Frijoles? Oh, Lawd. For the love of an unchapped ass.

Nancy Regan was right, son: *Just say no to drugs.*

Did Annie, with her stoic beauty, meet her demise by gastrointestinal massacre? Doubtful. But did Annie take her own life? If indeed that was the case, it's always possible that she took a poison or a drug. Particularly since there weren't any exterior signs of distress on her body. I mean, this ain't CSI Paris; it's not like they were running routine toxicology screenings in the 1800s.

But an absence of exterior abrasions has nothing to do with the possibility of her interior wounds. Whatever the reasoning—body image issues, illness, addiction (before we even called it that) depression, feeling like she was less than in a man's world, mental health issues (before we knew what they were), or a combination of all of the above—many have thought about or actually attempted to end their own lives. Annie would not have been the first . . . and she obviously would not have been the last.

chapter nine

Motive & Opportunity

Identifying possible suspects based on mounting evidence

The wall of stink hit me as soon as I opened the door of the Campus Safety department's Chevy Caprice. I worked hard to keep a straight face.

Once I became promoted to Watch Commander, I began to train the new Campus Safety hires. Read: everybody else who worked there was currently too busy/too lazy to do it, so they got the student labor involved. On this particular night, I had two trainees riding along. We were on the graveyard shift, and after walking them around the campus, we jumped into the white Chevy Caprice. Immediately when we closed the car doors, I realized there was a horrific smell in the air. I had absolutely no idea what it was, but it was disgustingly unpleasant and mysteriously undefinable.

It was early winter, after Christmas. So, it was pretty chilly, even in LA. I remember putting my window halfway down so I could take a breath of fresh air, but I was almost freezing to death, becoming an ice cube in about thirty seconds. I reached over and cranked the heat in the Caprice up and put all the windows down. Nobody said a word, and (back then) I really didn't want to point out something that might embarrass me or make me look even semi-unprofessional. I decided the risk was too great that the smell might be one of my trainees. I continued to ignore the stench and attempted to stay focused on the task at hand, but it was beyond awkward.

We drove around talking lightly with small conversations about things at school and things related to campus safety. I thought about all the *Moonlighting* episodes where Maddie and David sat in the car with binoculars during a stakeout or drove around LA arguing. Law enforcement, in its various forms, tended to consist of no shortage of time in the car.

But all the while, my nose was absolutely annihilated by the smell of this, and I couldn't believe nobody else smelled this horrific rich scent of something completely ripe and nasty. At every chance possible, I parked the Caprice and we got out and walked. But when we had to get in the car, I was mentally psyching myself up.

Finally, I couldn't take it. I decided I could be very unspecific and if the smell was a bodily smell, no one would really have to admit it. I said, "Do you guys smell that gnarly smell?"

Immediately, Steve, one of my trainees, jumped in and blurted out in relief: "Oh, thank God you finally said something!" He put his jacket up over his nose.

I looked at him and realized his eyes were watering. Looking in the rearview mirror, I realized Ramona had been breathing into her polo shirt the whole time.

She had pulled it up to the bridge of her nose and used her glasses to secure it from slipping. "I'm kinda nauseous," she whimpered.

All right. Time for a four-alarm, deep dive investigation with all hands on deck. We had to solve this case, and we needed all the clues we could gather. I threw the Caprice into park, and we all got out.

"Do you think we hit roadkill?" asked Steve.

Reasonable question, except we were in the midsize city of Azusa, California, on the border of Glendora, and it seemed unlikely. Nevertheless, we all walked around the Caprice and inspected the tires.

Ramona, looking pale even in the moonlight, suggested we look in the trunk.

Before I could interject or decide, Steve scrambled to the rear of the vehicle and popped it open. He jumped backward several feet and put his forearm to his nose. "Gahh!" he cried out.

Part of me just wanted to run away, felt the fight or flight starting to kick in, but I fought the desire to run, and, with a quasi-shaky voice, I asked, "Do we need to call for backup, Steve?"

Steve shook his head, still buried in his forearm.

Ramona stood frozen by the passenger side door. "WHAT IS IT? IS IT A DEAD BODY?" she screamed. Her jacket sleeves were pulled down over her hands, which she cupped over her face.

Just then it dawned on me. Gus.

Gus was Campus Safety's oldest employee, and he rarely had an actual working shift anymore, but he was always playing jokes on new hires. And apparently on me. I knew he was planning to play the traditional Campus Safety department initiation joke later, but whatever this was appeared to be the add-on, the "gift with purchase."

I pulled my shirt up over my nose, too, and kept a safe distance as I slowly inched my way to the rear of the vehicle and peered into the open trunk. Rows and rows of open tubs were laid out in the trunk. In the moonlight, I could tell whatever was in the tubs was dark in color and mushy looking, like Play-Doh. "What *IS* that?" I asked.

Steve edged forward, closer to the trunk again, grabbed my Maglight off my Sally Browne, and switched it on. A beam of light revealed the label on one of the containers. *"BeeJay Bait Co. Inc. Channel Catfish*

Bait: Blood Formula" was printed on the tub, or should I say *tubs plural*. There were seven double rows of the stuff, fourteen tubs in total, all with the lids off. The logo was a lovely whiskered catfish with its mouth wrapped around the tail of a fish. I would have loved to be there at that marketing meeting and be a fly on the wall when they solidified the decision on the agreed-upon logo.

"It's fishing bait," said Steve. "This stuff is NASTY!"

Well, no explanation needed. We were mere feet from a dumpster, so I instructed Ramona to grab three pairs of gloves from the glove compartment.

We spent the next ten minutes removing the tubs, but the smell seemed to be saturated into the velour seats of the Caprice, and it seemed to have seeped into the vents. It dawned on me that having the heat on probably didn't help keep the smell at bay; in fact, the heat most likely enhanced the power of the odorous substance. I made the executive decision to abandon the Caprice for the evening and have us finish the shift on foot.

Oddly, neither Ramona or Steve asked any questions as to why or how the blood bait got there. Novices. I, of course, had my suspicions now that I had remembered Gus' propensity for these types of shenanigans.

Our last patrol stop of the night was the science building called the "Wing Science Center," which was infused with an oppressively suffocating formaldehyde odor. It was the grand finale, Gus' masterpiece initiation ritual into the Campus Safety family ... a preplanned surprise, of sorts, waiting for Ramona and Steve inside the Wings Science Center.

Only the chief had the key to the cadaver room, and as watch commander that night, the chief's supersized set of keys jangled from their clasp on my Sally Browne with each step of my well-worn work Hi-Tec boots.

"Frank one, what's your ten twenty-one?" The scratch of the radio filled the crisp night air. Graveyard shift, appropriately.

I cleared my throat and pressed the mic on my Motorola. "Approaching area six." I could hear the self-admitted hideous sound of my voice echoing across the parking lot.

"Ten-four," responded dispatch in a nasally sounding tone. Welcome back to the '90s, people. This was our version of campus-cop GPS.

Rounding the corner of the science building, I grabbed the keys from my Sally Browne. The set filled my entire hand. In the dark, I fumbled around clumsily, finally switching my Maglite on so I could search for the key. It was stamped with a unique symbol engraved on top. Boom. Found it.

I slid the key into the lock and turned the double dead bolt to the right, with extra firm pressure, the way I'd been trained. I pulled the heavy door open with a firm yank. The chill overtook me suddenly, an Arctic blast; the wind whistled around me like I was an Alaskan Husky in the Iditarod Trail Dog Sled Race.

No one spoke.

Reluctantly, I stepped into the quasi-meat locker and shined my flashlight around the mint-green subway tiled room.

Stainless steel was the furniture palate of choice for this design project. Small shiny scales (organ-weighing devices) were suspended politely from the ceiling. There were two autopsy tables with raised edges to catch spills of God-only-knew-what kinds of bodily fluids. Hoses were hung above said tables with care, in hopes that Dr. Deathwash soon would be there.

A mint-green tiled floor was twinning the mint-green walls, save for the circular drainage cutouts. Like a foggy haze of Old Spice trying to cover up cigarette breath, hospital-grade cleaning products attempted to disguise the unique and sickly-sweet odor of decomposed and preserved death. A copious amount of formaldehyde did its best to preserve the hidden bodily treasures. It was still silent, except for our footsteps and the sound of our pounding hearts inside our heads. Even though I knew what was coming, the vibe still registered as "creepy."

Flashing the Maglite around, it was impossible to avoid the general feeling that some industrial designer for the building had picked a universal medical motif they liked to call "Doublemint Gum." ("Double your pleasure" surrounded by all green tiles. "Double your fun" as my stomach flipped from the wretched stench of death and disinfectant.) The only thing blatantly missing was that oh-so-coveted clean and refreshing minty taste.

Due to a lack of funding for the typical morgue "body drawers," gurneys on wheels holding lumpy white sheets lined the back wall. I found it interesting that there were sheets. People's naked bodies were under there. Was it really a goal, at this point, to harbor privacy?

My inner dialogue was interrupted when suddenly one of the sheets began moving and sat straight up and yelled "WELCOME!" Ramona spun around on her heels and let out a scream better than Janet Leigh in *Psycho*. Steve screamed, too, and jumped backward with such force that he knocked his head on one of the scales. He batted at it like a punching bag, clearly terrified.

Gus ripped the sheet off his body, cracking up. His beer belly jiggled, and his red Ronald McDonald hair stood straight out from static electricity. He was laughing too hard to even get himself and his beer belly up and off the gurney. It was tradition that we "christen" all new hires with a "welcome initiation" scare of some sort, in the cadaver room, and this was quite possibly Gus' favorite pastime in the whole world.

As Ramona and Steve tried to regain their composure, I pointed at Gus. "You. You're the only one who could have been responsible for the disgusting fish bait in the Caprice."

Gus smiled wryly and put his right hand on his heart then bowed his head. "Guilty as charged, your honor," he said.

Case closed. Apparently, it was Mr. Boddy, in the Caprice, with the blood bait.

"Oh, well, super, that's super." I nodded. "'Cause the Caprice is ready to be driven to the carwash, where *you* can figure out how to get that stench out of there." I tossed him the keys. "Have fun!"

Suddenly Gus stopped chuckling so hard, realizing he hadn't planned on having to deal with the fallout. He shifted gears and tried to get serious, asking the trainees a few review questions. He nodded and would interrupt here and there to tell a story or two with his larger-than-life, jovial voice and gestures.

I meandered around the chilly room and studied those lumpy sheets for a series of seconds as Gus chin-wagged. I'd been in here so many times before, but it hadn't dawned on me that the sheets were simply covers. No need for blankets or warmth; those human needs were over. *These* sheets were simply for draping, concealing. Sheets offering respect for the dead; sheets offering dignity. Sheets prevent the body from being revealed in an indisposed state.

Sheets . . . holding *secrets* underneath. Like the keys in my hand, under the sheets one could get access to information. One could discover the answers. With the unveiling of the sheet, one could unlock the possibility of solving the mystery.

"Let's go, Carlton!" said Gus, tossing the sheet in the laundry bin. He had successfully made it off the gurney without injuring himself, so that was a win.

Long after the body of the mysterious girl found drowned in the Seine was laid to rest, Dr. James Elam realized he was going to need an educational model for his CPR technique. He reached out to the Laerdal toy company to build him a lifelike rubber doll with faux lungs and arteries. Because Laerdal almost lost his son tragically to drowning, he was passionate about the project. He built the model, and when it came time for the doll to have a face, he recalled the copy of the calm and beautiful death mask his family had hanging in their living room. Annie's face became the face of the CPR doll, Resusci Annie.

And so began Resusci Annie's life 2.0, in teaching others how to give the chance to live the life she didn't have.

And eventually, Annie taught others to give life . . . she had been reborn.

chapter ten

Partners & Squads

Sharing resources and expertise as a community

*A*shirtless guy with an epic mullet and cutoff jean shorts (AKA jorts) whizzed by on rollerblades, a transistor radio balanced on his shoulder.

I was busy doing up the Velcro on my rollerblades and preparing to fly down the path at Redondo Beach with all the peeps. My top speed was about three and a half MPH. This ensured I'd be passed by all sorts of colorful, half-dressed individuals. Just people following the concept of *you do you*.

Down the path toward Seaside Lagoon, a group of barefoot kids played double Dutch to "The Breaks" by Kurtis Blow, which was bumping from a nearby lowrider.

Driving out to the beach by myself to rollerblade was my version of "doing me" in college. Carrying the old YMCA torch at APU, I procured a membership at the local 24 Hour Fitness. Once again, I joined the chain gang of participants married to the printed, neon-pink aerobics fitness class schedule. Step Aerobics, HIT Aerobics, Power Sculpt, the list went on. But every now and then, I wasn't feeling it and took advantage of the optimal Southern California weather, opting for outside activities to battle my freshman fifteen.

On one trip to Redondo Beach, I witnessed a *very* large woman walk onto the sand, by herself, and disrobe. Removing her sundress, she revealed a thong bikini underneath. She tossed her dress casually onto her towel and walked toward the water. Under her arm, she carried a neon yellow innertube. Headed to the shore, she flopped, belly first, onto the tube and began paddling out. As if she did it every day. I mean, as if she didn't have a care in the world.

I watched this woman just *let go* and utterly *relax*. She closed her eyes, let her limbs go limp, and she *rested*. Her face was turned to the side and her jaw was open just a little bit, as if she were dreaming. The bottom of her "swimming costume" disappeared in her butt crack. She couldn't have cared less. Then after a while, I watched her flip over and stretch onto her back, limbs outstretched, and float like a starfish on the water. She effortlessly basked in the enjoyment of the buoyancy.

Seeing grown women completely and wholeheartedly relax like that in a swimsuit is a rare thing for me. What I have seen a lot of, however, is women who act just like me around the pool or a beach. We're insecure and self-conscious, yanking on our swimming costumes, adjusting our boobs and our asses, covering our cellulite, making sure everything is tucked in . . . smoothing out any wonky bits, confirming we are positioned and situated "just right" on our lounge chairs to avoid any unwanted accidental flashings or wardrobe malfunctions.

You know what I realized that day on the beach? I felt jealous.

Jealous that the woman had the self-confidence to totally lean into relaxation in public. I have never experienced that sense of freedom at that level. In private, yes. But in public? That takes a serious set of balls that I generally didn't have. Yes, I was jealous indeed. Jealous she displayed pure surrender to her own personal fulfillment, regardless of her surroundings.

The only experience of my own I could equate to that type of surrender was my baptism at age eight. A public display of relaxation, oddly enough, through the "divine dunk." Baptism, we were assured, would seal the deal that we would be dipped down into the water as one person and raised to new life as another. Sounded good to me. I was all in. I was about to become not just Christian but *Christian Plus*. Add to cart.

On the day of my baptism, I arrived as instructed, ten minutes before the service, wearing my Michael Jackson *Thriller* concert T-shirt and carrying my towel. Sidebar: Had I been to the Michael Jackson *Thriller* concert? Negative, my dudes. But I had a mom who (when she wasn't at her booth selling earthquake preparedness kits) could moonlight as a bargain hunter at the De Anza Flea Market like a boss.

I met up with Mrs. Banks, the church secretary, in the choir rectory. "Hi, are you Amy?" she asked. "Randy and Gerri's daughter?" She glanced quickly at the *Thriller* T-shirt and blinked.

"Yes," I answered. She wrote something very important down on her clipboard. Then it dawned on me she looked just like Jane Fonda in *9 to 5* with her long-sleeved lilac midi dress with the high neck, nude pantyhose, and Naturalizers. She also had the same type of glasses as Jane, hanging on a chain dangling around her neck.

We climbed the stairs up to the choir rehearsal loft. The choir robes and sashes were all hung neatly on four rounders. I followed Mrs. Banks into a small practice room, and she propped the door open with a wedge of lumber. She sauntered over to the old piano and pulled the cover over top of the ivory keys. I guess she was afraid I might be inspired to play a little pre-baptism "Chopsticks."

There was a large Moses basket sitting next to the piano, and she pointed to it. "You may put your change of clothes there," she instructed. "When I leave the room, please feel free to strip down to your undergarments and put on your baptismal robes." Then she gingerly picked up a garment bag hanging in the corner. Unzipping the bag, she proudly displayed a shiny white polyester robe that was surely not going to be see-through when one descended into the water.

Mrs. Banks carefully folded the garment bag, as if she were a soldier folding the US flag at the Tomb of the Unknown Soldier at Arlington National Cemetery. She placed it carefully on the piano bench and turned to me.

"Any questions?" she inquired and cupped her hand to her ear leaning toward me slightly. I shook my head. "Very well then. Just open the door when you're ready, and I'll take you to the baptistry to meet Reverend Melvin." I nodded.

Mrs. Banks moved the wooden wedge, dimmed the light switch on the wall, and closed the door. I took a deep breath and paused for a moment to acknowledge that this was the last time I would be my unbaptized little self. I inspected the robe, which looked different in the dimmer light. Its white glimmer illuminated like a Christmas tree. I bowed my head and said a little prayer. Then I changed, put my things into the Moses basket, and opened the door.

Mrs. Banks stood there, crossing her arms over her clipboard. "All right," she said with a hushed voice. "The service has started, and Reverend Melvin will be in the baptistry in three minutes. I'll take you down and have you wait on the side of the stairs for him to signal you into the water."

I was about to ask her what I should do with my towel, but she smashed her index finger against her lips and shook her head. I had forgotten she said that the service had already started, and I bet there was a no-talking-from-this-point-on type of a rule. She guided me down the hall and then angled my shoulders to face a small staircase. I could just see Reverend Melvin descending the opposite staircase and into the water.

He was wearing the weirdest getup I had ever seen. I wasn't quite sure if it was a set of galoshes with rubber pants, or some fisherman's overalls with boots attached. I don't know what kind of Baptist fashion exclusive it was, but I was quite certain you weren't going to be able to find that outfit at Ross Dress for Less. As he maneuvered himself through the water, which was basically a giant bathtub as far as I could tell, he raised his arms above the water (which was about waist-deep on his frame), and in his enormous hands, he held a big leather Bible, as if it were the *Lion King* baby, Simba.

Through the sliding baptismal door, I could just hear the music pastor, Bill Darling, start conducting the organist on "What a Friend We Have in Jesus." Reverend Melvin turned me and smiled widely. I could see his perfect dentures reassuring me that everything would be okay.

"Hello, my child!" he said in a soft voice, indicating we could talk now, but not too loudly, as the rest of the church service was going on right on the other side of the baptismal door.

"Hi," I whispered.

"Go ahead and place your towel on the stand right there." He motioned toward a marble pillar to my right.

Oh, okay. That's what I was going to ask Mrs. Banks. I did as I was told.

"Now," he instructed, "come on down the stairs here, and don't be afraid. There's nothing to worry about, and the water is nice and warm. Just come in and you'll see. I will help you get onto the stool so you can share your confession of faith with the church body." Which was the part I was least looking forward to.

He outstretched his arm, and I could see a thick gold chain bracelet attached to his wrist. For some reason, that was surprising to me.

I reached out and grabbed his giant hand. It felt rough, calloused, and supersized. I looked at my hand in his for a moment. My fingers looked like Vienna sausages. I almost got the giggles but pulled myself together.

I stuck my left foot out and dipped my toe in the water. He was right, it was nice and warm. Placing my foot down onto the first step, I noticed some leg hair and scolded myself for not trying my mom's Epilady prior to this moment. I raised my right foot and placed it on the second step. I watched as my robe began to fall into the water, ever lowering into the pool right along with my body.

As promised, Reverend Melvin helped me onto the stool. I noted the baptismal door was actually more of a sliding window as opposed to a door. Kind of like a fast-food drive-through.

I almost started giggling to myself again as I pictured Reverend Melvin sliding the door open and me leaning over and yelling into the microphone, "Do you want fries with that?"

I stood there, all robed up, in the Rolls Royce of Baptist Jacuzzis, and trusted the process. Reverend Melvin had one hand on the small of my back, one hand on his big Bible, which he set up on a little plastic podium right in front of where I stood on the stool.

The choir was wrapping up—I could tell by the way the song got slower.

Reverend Melvin turned to me, smiled again, and winked. "Ready?" he asked. His breath smelled like coffee and Poligrip. Before I could answer, he slid the baptistry drive-through window open with a bang and clicked it into place on the side of the wall unit.

I stared out into the congregation and instantly switched into panic mode. Suddenly, my heart was pounding. I could see my parents, I could see my choir teacher, my Sunday school teachers, my peers' parents, and the choir singers who basically looked like the members of Kool & the Gang as they shuffled and scurried to find their seats, scattering throughout the pews.

Reverend Melvin reached out and grabbed the microphone, adjusting it with his hand so it was pointed downward, closer to me. He bent over and joyfully addressed the audience. Next, he read a scripture passage from that big Simba-Bible and introduced me to the congregation, most of whom already knew me. Then he asked me some previously rehearsed questions about my faith.

I answered all the questions and proceeded to launch into my confession of faith including the fact that I had officially accepted Christ while praying in my closet, at which the congregation collectively chuckled. *What?* I didn't get what was so funny—it's not like I said I was on the toilet, for the love of Peter Pan.

Then, Reverend Melvin closed his leather Bible and smiled and said, "Having been commissioned by Jesus Christ and granted authority by Him..."

This was my cue. I knew what to do here. I put my hand over my nose and plugged it. He reached out and put his left hand over my nose-plugging hand, so I got double nose block coverage.

Reverend Melvin switched suddenly into an authoritative voice: deep and bold, and *exactly* what I imagined The Lord's voice sounded like: "I now, by the testimony of your word and confession of your faith, baptize you in the name of the Father, Son, and Holy Ghost."

I noted that he sounded exactly like Skeletor from the Masters of the Universe commercials.

At any rate, "Father, Son, and Holy Ghost" was my other cue. I took a massive breath and held it. Squeezing my eyes closed, I could feel Reverend Melvin gently tilt me backward. My first instinct was to resist, but for some reason I can't identify, I surrendered and let my body go limp. At once, I was underwater, and suddenly it was as if someone smashed the pause button, as three seconds felt like three minutes.

In my mind, under the water, it was like the *Moonlighting* episode where Maddie Hayes, the Blue Moon Shampoo's original down girl, sees quick glimpses of her life from previous episodes, flashing before her eyes. The scenes flipped by quickly, like clicking through a viewfinder toy, or your Aunt Patsy's slide carousel containing approximately 999 vacation photos from her trip to the Maldives.

That's what I felt happened to me under the water, but almost too quickly to realize it. *Flash!* Cheating off Carly Wineburger's math test in the second grade. *Flash!* Holding my newborn brother for the first time. *Flash!* Letting the seaweed wrap around my ankles as the waves crashed at my feet on Santa Cruz Beach. *Flash!*

The next thing I knew, I was pulled out of the water before it could really register that I'd been in it. The deed was done. I was part of the Baptized Squad. Signed, sealed, delivered, I'm yours. I was in the club. No need for that towel after all; just toss me the Members Only jacket. I was part of the crew. I gasped and coughed, involuntarily spitting a little bit.

"Raised to New Life!" cried Reverend Melvin into the microphone. I could hear the cheers and whistles from the audience as Reverend Melvin turned my shoulders back to the stairwell and let me wade over to Mrs. Banks, who was standing on the top step grabbing my towel off the marble pillar. I trudged up the stairs in the wet robe, with wet hair dripping down my back, and I suddenly wondered how many had gone before me, and if they had to scrub a murky film of Aqua Net from the baptistry after each person. This was, after all, the 1980s.

I did feel different. I can't explain it. It was significant. Even if not because of the actual event but maybe just in the pomp and circumstance of it all. Perhaps it was the symbolism, the feeling of initiation. Maybe that's where I first got all caught up in the enigma of tangible rituals, which is something I practice in my stepwork today. Maybe it was the time-warped hyper-speed highlight reel of an eight-year-old's life. Whatever it was, I felt a part of something bigger than myself. I was on a team, I had partners, I was in the club. And I was *all in*. Purchase completed.

So back to jealousy of that woman at Redondo Beach, surrendering in self-acceptance. That woman's confidence was so moving for me that it stuck with me. I recalled the memory of her beautiful surrender and my subsequent jealousy years later with my psychiatrist when I was diagnosed with ADHD.

I told him, "Not only am I not confident enough to be like her, but I don't think I could lay there with my thoughts for so long."

My shrink puffed on his Sherlock Holmes pipe stuffed with Captain Black tobacco and simply said, "Well, that's often one of the first signs for girls with ADHD. The assumption that you can't do something. It's the presupposition that you can't, based on previous experiences with an inability to focus. That's where the negative self-talk begins. Or begins and repeats at infinitum, I should say."

Why I didn't listen to this man sooner is another mystery, for another book.

It's also been explained to me (and has been my experience) that gender stereotypes have played a role in the underdiagnosis of girls with ADHD because females presented our symptoms differently from males growing up. The social expectations were set up differently for girls, so many of us went undiagnosed in the 1980s and '90s because diagnostic criteria were originally based on hyperactive boys.

For me and many other undiagnosed girls, the "hyperactive" branch of the ADHD tree presented itself as impulsivity (remember the Spanish book cartoons?), having a *chatterbox personality* and/or the *heightened dramatic personality*, and later, alcohol addiction. But my ADHD also presented itself by way of anxiety: panic attacks, flooding of adrenaline, and fight-or-flight mentalities. Which, interestingly, was often categorized by what caregivers and educators referred to as a "rebellious" personality. (Ergo, my panic attack with Annie, the CPR dummy, and subsequent refusal to participate.)

The "inattentive" branch of the ADHD tree often presented for me in the lack of attention in school due to boredom. Remember the "We Don't Give a Shit" group? The inability to read a room, not thinking things through (my super warp speed speech in Japan), and embarrassing kerfuffles (yelling "PUBES!" at the junior high dance) were all part of ADHD. The disorganization and challenges with problem-solving when wandering through the streets of San Jose looking for the driver's ed class are a perfect example of my struggle with executive functioning. This commonly occurs in kids with ADHD and manifests as difficulty with goal-oriented activities.

Having as many children as I do certainly spotlights the presentations of my symptoms. Juggling ten constantly changing schedules, the planning of everything from school projects and activities to vacations and holidays and the details pertaining, the filling out of endless forms, dentist and doctor's appointments, outgrown clothes and shoes, managing the purging of old things and the implementation of the new, the general and constant plate-spinning of ten lives present an ongoing challenge.

Ultimately, being diagnosed with ADHD was profoundly empowering for me. Connecting the awkward puzzle pieces has given me agency over my life in a way I never thought possible. Once you know the suspects, the locations, and the weapons you're dealing with, you can begin the process of solving the case and managing your symptoms.

Eventually, it's as if you're running your special magnifying glass over explanations written in invisible ink.

At the end of my first book, *Eternally Expecting*, I shared about my diagnosis of a heart condition called cardiomyopathy. After years of hearing the heartbeats of my growing babies through the ultrasound machine, I finally became familiar with the sound of my own. With this in mind, I was fascinated to discover an additional treasure during my deep dive to the ocean floor for this book: the sound of the beating heart in the introduction of "Smooth Criminal" was Michael Jackson's very own heartbeat. Specifically recorded for "Smooth Criminal," Michael's heartbeat is now forever immortalized. *Invincible*. Which, by the way, was the name of one of Michael's earlier albums. Contained in that album is a photo of Michael waist-deep near a waterfall, wearing a set of angel wings. Signifying, of course, that his spirit will soar and live on in the afterlife.

At the risk of sounding morbid, Michael Jackson is dead. Annie, pulled from the Seine River, is dead. The irony of the cadaver room, where the bodies were housed, was that it was located in the Wings Science Center. The bodies, the containers of the soul, were just mysteries lying under the sheets, but the death, or the proverbial wings, provided the escape route—the fast pass to the soul's next chapter.

In death, Annie got her wings and became eternal.

epilogue

Hook 'Em & Book 'Em

Arresting perpetrators based on probable cause

Without struggle or challenge, imagine what a boring 1980s movie or plotline you'd be faced with watching. No entertaining, wonderful, beautiful '80s movie is adversity-free. Think about it. How would anyone begin to market the movie trailer to advertise that someone had a perfect life, and thanks for watching. Yawn.

On the contrary, it's a hallmark of a great plotline to contain highs and lows, challenges and successes, victories and triumphs, disappointments and defeats. And this isn't a one-hit wonder like "Bust a Move" by Young MC. This is a cycle, repeating itself many times across the span of a life.

If we deny our life's challenges, avoid self-discovery, if we pretend these concepts don't exist, it's been my experience they will haunt the house, like a ghost on an episode of *Unsolved Mysteries* or those hitchhiking phantoms in the mirror at the end of the Disneyland Haunted Mansion ride.

The mystery of my ongoing awkwardness and watershed moment with Annie the CPR dummy has been solved. What was once a cold case has now been closed, at least my common threads tied to her. The confidential file has been opened and inspected.

Very few mysteries are cut and dry, predictable story lines. One peek inside a *Clue* game picked up at a garage sale or the De Anza Flea Market will reveal this theory. Pieces of scratch paper and old detective notepads from games nights past instantly demonstrate this idea. You see the scribble, the chicken scratch, the scrawled notes that are more illegible than a prescription pad. Arrows and diagrams, question marks.

Our process is often a jumbled, unorthodox mess. It's like that game many of us played as kids in the swimming pool called "Marco, Polo." It seems like we blindly swim around, fumbling around, listening for a clue. Occasionally we hit the wall. Sometimes, we hit dead ends. Just when we think we're on the right path, the direction of the voice changes, and we must pivot. We tug on our ill-fitting swimming costumes, and at times, we're overwhelmed, and it feels like drowning.

Over time, we learn to just embrace whichever awkward character we become, and hopefully we allow that character to morph, grow, and change. We get in the game. We expect some twists and turns. Like Maddie and David in *Moonlighting*, we leap off the roof and into the pool. We learn to swim.

We arrest the idea that it all needs to make sense while we're in it. And we surrender to the messy, to the confusing and frustrating process. Sometimes this comes easily, and other times it's hard-fought. We start practicing setting aside the black-and-white and instead practice looking for peace amid the gray. Beauty in the mess.

We just follow the clues, as awkward as they may seem.

ETERNALLY
awkward
Activity Pages

Hidden Pictures

Help Annie find the hidden objects, and circle them!

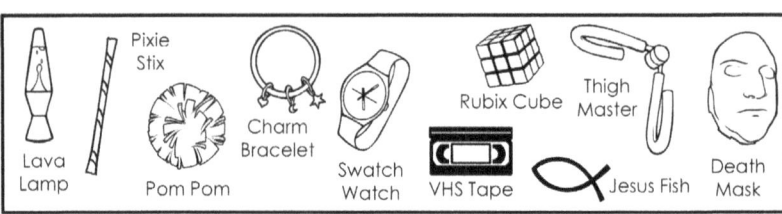

- Lava Lamp
- Pixie Stix
- Pom Pom
- Charm Bracelet
- Swatch Watch
- Rubix Cube
- VHS Tape
- Thigh Master
- Jesus Fish
- Death Mask

WORD SEARCH

FIND AND CIRCLE ALL THE WORDS FROM THE LIST BELOW

CLUE	PARIS	AQUANET	RETAINER
MOONLIGHTING	PITFALL	FROGGER	JORTS
ANNIE	PUBES	NINTENDO	THRILLER
EPILADY	PERM	SCORPIONS	VELCRO
BOOMBOX	VHS	SIZZLER	ROLLERBLADES

```
T S F X L R T E W C Z M F G P
H F C R W O B S F L A E Y P U
R N R O O K K P V U N E S P B
I I Y O R L P Y K E N P S E E
L N N U G P L A V L I I I R S
L T D Z V G I E R A E L Z M P
E E G B H E E O R I H A Z J I
R N Q T S S G R N B S D L O T
W D B O O M B O X S L Y E R F
S O M J S X Z V Z W I A R T A
M O O N L I G H T I N G D S L
L Z P U A O U D M J J H R E L
E K A Q U A N E T L U E Z W S
R E T A I N E R T W H I X Z W
D E M I L X E C V E L C R O F
```

CROSSWORD PUZZLE

DOWN:

1. Original 1980s true crime show hosted by Robert Stack.

2. A prime-time detective show, starring Cybil Shepperd and Bruce Willis, that aired on ABC from 1985 to 1989.

3. A colloquial term for one who works and travels with a carnival or circus.

4. The 1980s new wave band just as famous for their front man's iconic hairstyle as their song, I Ran (So Far Away).

5. An exercise device marketed by TV personality Suzanne Somers in the late 1980s.

ACROSS:

1. The "whodunnit" board game, where players attempt to solve a fictional murder.

2. A vintage telephone design with a circular dial that requires the caller to turn the dial for each digit of the phone number.

3. Michael Jackson's 1989 hit that featured a chorus that included the phrase, "Annie, are you okay?"

4. The Japanese word for cherry blossom.

5. The brand of aerosol hairspray famous for cementing the sky-high hairstyles of the 1980s.

M.A.S.H.

SPOUSE
1. _____
2. _____
3. _____
4. _____

JOBS
1. _____
2. _____
3. _____
4. _____

CITY
1. _____
2. _____
3. _____
4. _____

PETS
1. _____
2. _____
3. _____
4. _____

KIDS
1. _____
2. _____
3. _____
4. _____

VEHICLE
1. _____
2. _____
3. _____
4. _____

GAME RULES:

You will find the directions on how to play the M.A.S.H. game on the answers page of this activity book.

MAD LIB

One player acts as the reader and asks the other players, who haven't seen the story, to fill in the blanks with adjectives, nouns, exclamations, colors, adverbs, and more. These words are inserted into the blanks and then the story is read aloud to hilarious results. There are no winners or losers, only laughter.

The year was 1988. I was wearing a _____ and a _____. I ran my fingers
                                     (item of clothing)   *(item of clothing)*
through my _____ and took a sip of my _____. "Who's That Girl" by
           (name of hairstyle)   *(name of beverage)*
Madonna was playing _____ on the transistor radio when _____
                    (adverb)   *(name of person in room)*
began to tell the _____ legend of the drowned girl in Paris in 1880s. The
                 (adjective)
only_____ truth we know is she was dragged _____ out of the River Seine.
    (adjective)   *(adverb)*
Nobody knew who she was or how she got there. Theories began swirling around like a bad

_____. This was the _____ drama since
    (noun)   *(adjective)*
_____ was it self-inflicted_____? Maybe it was a
(name of a Shakespearean play)   *(name of a manner of death)*
jilted lover from _____ or was she assaulted by a jealous rival and her partner in
                 (name of a place)
crime, _____? To this day, no one is sure of who committed this
       (name of past or present celebrity)
_____ crime. No headway was ever made in solving this _____ dastardly
 (adjective)   *(adjective)*
_____ connundrum. Whether the woman was a prostitute or a
(name of a crime)
_____ , one thing remains a _____ and timeless truth:
(name of profession)   *(adjective)*
crime doesn't _____ and francs don't float.
              (verb)

HANGMAN

Key Word:

Directions:

One player thinks of a word or phrase; the others try to guess what it is one letter at a time. The player draws a number of dashes equivalent to the number of letters in the word. If a guessing player suggests a letter that occurs in the word, the other player fills in the blanks with that letter in the right places. If the word does not contain the suggested letter, the other player draws one element of a man on a noose. Those elements include the head, torso, right arm, left arm, right leg, and left leg. As the game progresses, a segment of the gallows and of a victim is added for every suggested letter not in the word. The number of incorrect guesses before the game ends is up to the players, but completing a character in a noose provides a minimum of six wrong answers until the game ends. The first player to guess the correct answer thinks of the word for the next game.

I W_ S_ INN_CENT!

WHY ME?

SUPER FUN HAIR MATCH

MATCH THE HAIR TO THE FACES OF '80S STARS

CUT OUT MASK

1. Color and cut out mask. (Add hair if you want, get creative, go crazy!)
2. Attach a ruler to the back with duct tape so you can hold it up.
3. Take it to strange and wonderful places.
4. Take a picture of yourself holding the mask up to a face (your own face is fine) and tag **@amylizharrison** on Instagram.

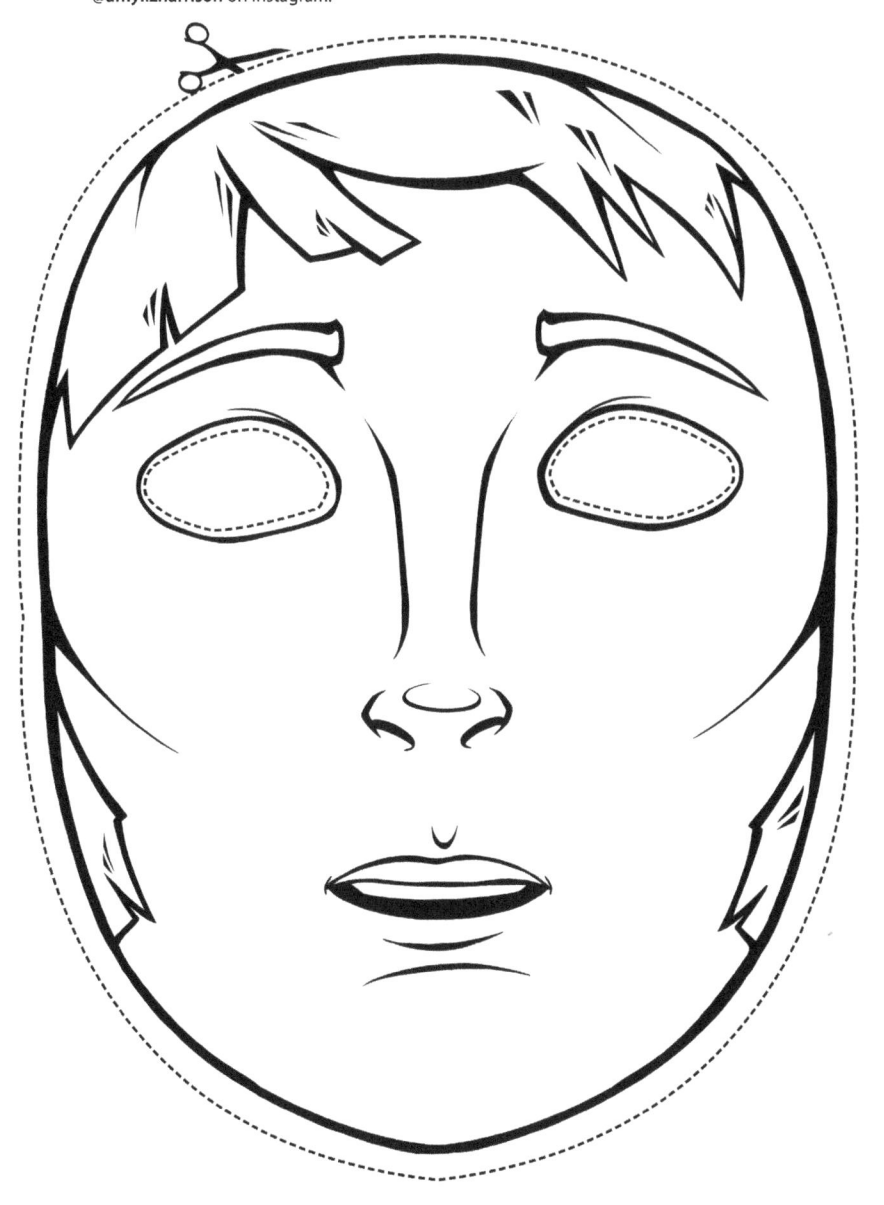

ANSWERS & INSTRUCTIONS

WORD SEARCH

```
T S F X L R T E W C Z M F G P
H F C R W O B S F L A E Y P U
R N R O K K P V U N E S P B
I I Y O R L P Y K E N P S E E
L N N U G P L A V L I I R S
L T D Z V G I E R A E L Z M P
E E G B H E E O R I H A Z J I
R N Q T S S G R N B S D L O T
W D B O O M B O X S L Y E R F
S O M J S X Z V Z W I A R T A
M O O N L I G H T I N G D S L
L Z P U A O U D M J J H R E L
E K A Q U A N E T L U E Z W S
R E T A I N E R T W H I X Z W
D E M I L X E C V E L C R O F
```

CROSSWORD PUZZLE

Across / Down filled:
- CLUE
- ROTARYPHONE
- CROSSWORD
- PUZZLE
- SMOOTHCRIMINAL
- SAKURA
- AQUANET
- THIGH
- etc.

M.A.S.H.

Let's get a "CLUE" about what the future holds for you!

Directions:

1. Imagine the life of your dreams. Box by box, go through the categories and picture two of the very best things you can imagine in each category. Write those two things on any two blanks in that category box.
2. Repeat step 1, but with things from the life of your nightmares, filling in the rest of the blanks.
3. Put your pen down on the paper, and close your eyes. Start to draw your magic spiral, and stop whenever you want.
4. Open your eyes. Like a redwood tree sliced open, start at the outside of your spiral and count the number of rings. This is your magic number.
5. Starting at the "M" in MASH, count each letter, and then each choice, in the boxes. Count the rows with your pen until you hit your magic number. Then stop and cross out the choice in the box.
6. Repeat step 5, skipping over the choices that have already been marked or circled. (Circle a choice if it's the only one that hasn't been marked out in its category.)
7. Continue until every option is either circled or crossed out.
8. Read each of the circled options and you will see how MASH has magically predicted your future!

CAN WE TURN UP THE AC? I'VE BEEN GROPED BY 19 SCHOOL KIDS AND COUNTING, AND IT'S AS HOT AS BALLS. I'M SWEATING LIKE A WHORE IN CHURCH.
GO AHEAD AND COP A FEEL. TRUST ME: YOU'RE NOT THE FIRST, AND YOU DARN SURE WON'T BE THE LAST!
I'VE SEEN SOME THINGS. LET'S JUST SAY I'VE BEEN AROUND THE BLOCK...OOPS, ER, UH, I MEAN, I'VE BEEN AROUND THE SUITCASE.
LOOK, FOR THE LAST TIME, I AM SOBER. I DON'T NEED TO GO TO REHAB JUST BECAUSE I SMELL LIKE A VODKA DISTILLERY ALL THE TIME. SERIOUSLY!

DO YOU KISS YOUR MOTHER WITH THAT MOUTH? 'CAUSE, I'M GONNA BE STRAIGHT WITH YOU: YOU NEED TO GET YOURSELF SOME CHAPSTICK.
SEX, DRUGS, AND ROCK N' ROLL, MAN.
I SEE YOU CHECKING FOR MY BOOGERS. NO DICE. I'VE GOT THE CLEANEST NOSE IN ALL OF PARIS, THE BETTER TO SNIFF YOUR BUTTCRACK WITH, MY DEAR.
EXCUSE ME, COULD YOU TAKE A BREAK AND GO FIND A HAIR TIE? I CAN TASTE YOUR PERM.

About the Author

Before she was a sober mom of eight living in the suburbs of Seattle, Amy Liz Harrison grew up as a creative dreamer and Evangelical Christian kid in 1980s (read: pre-Google) Mountain View, California. She returned to her birthplace of Los Angeles to attend university then moved to Silicon Valley after graduation, where she married an Australian future airline executive six weeks later.

Grounded by life as a young tenth-grade teacher turned stay-at-home mom to four kids, Harrison watched her husband's career soar. He gained altitude, earning promotions and relocating the family. Meanwhile, Amy struggled with excess baggage. Depression, isolation, boredom, and a devastating crisis of faith led to extra glasses (or bottles) of wine and a platinum elite card-carrying membership to the Mommy Wine Club. Eventually, this lifestyle led to a shiny pair of silver bracelets—not Tiffany, mind you, but *handcuffs*—and incarceration at King County's largest hotel with non-optional exit privileges. Two trips to rehab and a supportive husband by her side set the foundation for a new journey.

Harrison has learned firsthand the dangers of failing to place the oxygen mask on herself before others. She is well aware some flights are turbulent, requiring a change in altitude and productive action steps to avoid a crash. Sorting through her past wreckage, coupled with countless hours of professional help, became her "black box," revealing an untreated ADHD diagnosis. Today, Harrison is fueled by the knowledge that by giving her recovery priority boarding, she can expect everything else in her life to fly first class.

Over a decade and four bonus biological babies later, Harrison has written two chuckle-inducing autobiographical books about her experiences with alcoholism and ADHD and coauthored an anthology. She is still married to the same Aussie, who remains supportive of her flight plan.

Lightning Source UK Ltd.
Milton Keynes UK
UKHW021835210422
401865UK00008B/1847